The Recruiting Officer

By
George Farquhar

ANODOS BOOKS
Candida Casa

George Farquhar (1677-1707)
Originally published in 1706
Editing, cover, and internal design by Alisdair MacNoravaich for Anodos Books.
Copyright © 2017 Anodos Books. All rights reserved.

Anodos Books
1c Kings Road
Whithorn
Newton Stewart
Dumfries & Galloway
DG8 8PP

Contents

DRAMATIS PERSONÆ.

MEN.

CAPTAIN PLUME	*Mr. Holman.*
JUSTICE BALANCE	*Mr. Murray.*
WORTHY	*Mr. Whitfield.*
SERJEANT KITE	*Mr. Knight.*
BULLOCK	*Mr. Fawcett.*
FIRST RECRUIT	*Mr. Munden.*
SECOND RECRUIT	*Mr. Emery.*
WELSH COLLIER	*Mr. Farley.*
CONSTABLE	*Mr. Thompson.*
CAPTAIN BRAZEN	*Mr. Lewis.*

WOMEN.

MELINDA	*Miss Chapman.*
ROSE	*Mrs. Gibbs.*
LUCY	*Mrs. Litchfield.*
SYLVIA	*Mrs. Johnson.*

SCENE—Shrewsbury.

1

ACT I.

SCENE I.

The Market Place.

Drum beats the Grenadier's March.——
Enter Serjeant Kite, *followed by* Thomas Appletree, Costar Pearmain,
and the Mob.

Kite. [*Making a Speech.*] If any gentlemen soldiers or others, have a mind to serve his majesty, and pull down the French king; if any 'prentices have severe masters, any children have undutiful parents; if any servants have too little wages, or any husband too much wife, let them repair to the noble Serjeant Kite, at the sign of the Raven, in this good town of Shrewsbury, and they shall receive present relief and entertainment.——[*Drum.*]——Gentlemen, I don't beat my drums here to insnare or inveigle any man; for you must know, gentlemen, that I am a man of honour: besides, I don't beat up for common soldiers; no, I list only grenadiers; grenadiers, gentlemen.——Pray, gentlemen, observe this cap—this is the cap of honour; it dubs a man a gentleman, in the drawing of a trigger; and he, that has the good fortune to be born six foot high, was born to be a great man—Sir, will you give me leave to try this cap upon your head?

Cost. Is there no harm in't? won't the cap list me?

Kite. No, no, no more than I can.—Come, let me see how it becomes you.

Cost. Are you sure there is no conjuration in it? no gunpowder plot upon me?

Kite. No, no, friend; don't fear, man.

Cost. My mind misgives me plaguily.—Let me see it—[*Going to put it on.*] It smells woundily of sweat and brimstone. Smell, Tummas.

Tho. Ay, wauns does it.

Cost. Pray, Serjeant, what writing is this upon the face of it?

Kite. The crown, or the bed of honour.

Cost. Pray now, what may be that same bed of honour?

3

Kite. Oh! a mighty large bed! bigger by half than the great bed at Ware —ten thousand people may lie in it together, and never feel one another.

Cost. My wife and I would do well to lie in't, for we don't care for feeling one another——But do folk sleep sound in this same bed of honour?

Kite. Sound! ay, so sound that they never wake.

Cost. Wauns! I wish again that my wife lay there.

Kite. Say you so! then I find, brother——

Cost. Brother! hold there friend; I am no kindred to you that I know of yet.—Lookye, serjeant, no coaxing, no wheedling, d'ye see—If I have a mind to list, why so—if not, why 'tis not so—therefore take your cap and your brothership back again, for I am not disposed at this present writing.—No coaxing, no brothering me, 'faith.

Kite. I coax! I wheedle! I'm above it, sir: I have served twenty campaigns ——but, sir, you talk well, and I must own that you are a man, every inch of you; a pretty, young, sprightly fellow!—I love a fellow with a spirit; but I scorn to coax; 'tis base; though I must say, that never in my life have I seen a man better built. How firm and strong he treads! he steps like a castle! but I scorn to wheedle any man—Come, honest lad! will you take share of a pot?

Cost. Nay, for that matter, I'll spend my penny with the best he that wears a head, that is, begging your pardon, sir, and in a fair way.

Kite. Give me your hand then; and now, gentlemen, I have no more to say but this—here's a purse of gold, and there is a tub of humming ale at my quarters—'tis the king's money, and the king's drink—he's a generous king, and loves his subjects—I hope, gentlemen, you won't refuse the king's health.

All Mob. No, no, no.

Kite. Huzza, then! huzza for the king, and the honour of Shropshire.

All Mob. Huzza!

Kite. Beat drum.

[*Exeunt, shouting.—Drum beating the Grenadier's March.*

Enter PLUME, *in a Riding Habit.*

Plume. By the Grenadier's march, that should be my drum, and by that shout, it should beat with success.—Let me see—four o'clock— [*Looking on his Watch.*] At ten yesterday morning I left London—an hundred and twenty miles in thirty hours is pretty smart riding, but nothing to the fatigue of recruiting.

Enter KITE.

Kite. Welcome to Shrewsbury, noble captain! from the banks of the Danube to the Severn side, noble captain! you're welcome.

Plume. A very elegant reception, indeed, Mr. Kite. I find you are fairly entered into your recruiting strain—Pray what success?

Kite. I've been here a week, and I've recruited five.

Plume. Five! pray what are they?

Kite. I have listed the strong man of Kent, the king of the gipsies, a Scotch pedlar, a scoundrel attorney, and a Welsh parson.

Plume. An attorney! wert thou mad? list a lawyer! discharge him, discharge him, this minute.

Kite. Why, sir?

Plume. Because I will have nobody in my company that can write; a fellow that can write, can draw petitions—I say this minute discharge him.

Kite. And what shall I do with the parson?

Plume. Can he write?

Kite. Hum? he plays rarely upon the fiddle.

Plume. Keep him, by all means—But how stands the country affected? were the people pleased with the news of my coming to town?

Kite. Sir, the mob are so pleased with your honour, and the justices and better sort of people, are so delighted with me, that we shall soon do your business——But, sir, you have got a recruit here, that you little think of.

Plume. Who?

Kite. One that you beat up for the last time you were in the country. You remember your old friend Molly, at the Castle?

Plume. She's not with child, I hope?

Kite. She was brought to-bed yesterday.

Plume. Kite, you must father the child.

Kite. And so her friends will oblige me to marry the mother.

Plume. If they should, we'll take her with us; she can wash, you know, and make a bed upon occasion.

Kite. Ay, or unmake it upon occasion. But your honour knows that I am married already.

Plume. To how many?

Kite. I can't tell readily—I have set them down here upon the back of the muster-roll. [*Draws it out.*] Let me see—*Imprimis*, Mrs. Shely Snikereyes; she sells potatoes upon Ormond key, in Dublin—Peggy Guzzle, the brandy woman at the Horse Guards, at Whitehall—Dolly Waggon, the carrier's daughter, at Hull—Mademoiselle Van Bottomflat, at the Buss—then Jenny Oakum, the ship-carpenter's widow, at Portsmouth; but I don't reckon upon her, for she was married at the same time to two lieutenants of marines, and a man of war's boatswain.

Plume. A full company—you have named five—come, make them half a dozen—Kite, is the child a boy, or a girl?

Kite. A chopping boy.

Plume. Then set the mother down in your list, and the boy in mine; enter him a grenadier, by the name of Francis Kite, absent upon furlow —I'll allow you a man's pay for his subsistence; and now, go comfort the wench in the straw.

Kite. I shall, sir.

Plume. But hold, have you made any use of your fortune-teller's habit since you arrived?

Kite. Yes, yes, sir; and my fame's all about the country for the most faithful fortune-teller that ever told a lie—I was obliged to let my landlord into the secret, for the convenience of keeping it so; but he is

6

an honest fellow, and will be faithful to any roguery that is trusted to him. This device, sir, will get you men, and me, money, which, I think, is all we want at present—But yonder comes your friend, Mr. Worthy —Has your honour any further commands?

Plume. None at present. [*Exit* KITE.] 'Tis indeed, the picture of Worthy, but the life is departed.

Enter WORTHY.

What, arms across, Worthy! methinks you should hold them open when a friend's so near—The man has got the vapours in his ears, I believe. I must expel this melancholy spirit.

Spleen, thou worst of fiends below,
Fly, I conjure thee, by this magic blow.

[*Slaps* WORTHY *on the Shoulder.*

Wor. Plume! my dear captain! welcome. Safe and sound returned!

Plume. I escaped safe from Germany, and sound, I hope, from London: you see I have lost neither leg, arm, nor nose. Then for my inside, 'tis neither troubled with sympathies, nor antipathies; and I have an excellent stomach for roast beef.

Wor. Thou art a happy fellow: once I was so.

Plume. What ails thee, man? no inundations nor earthquakes, in Wales, I hope? Has your father rose from the dead, and reassumed his estate?

Wor. No.

Plume. Then you are married, surely?

Wor. No.

Plume. Then you are mad, or turning quaker?

Wor. Come, I must out with it.——Your once gay, roving friend, is dwindled into an obsequious, thoughtful, romantic, constant coxcomb.

Plume. And pray, what is all this for?

Wor. For a woman.

Plume. Shake hands, brother. If you go to that, behold me as obsequious, as thoughtful, and as constant a coxcomb, as your worship.

7

Wor. For whom?

Plume. For a regiment—but for a woman! 'Sdeath! I have been constant to fifteen at a time, but never melancholy for one: and can the love of one bring you into this condition? Pray, who is this wonderful Helen?

Wor. A Helen, indeed! not to be won under ten years' siege; as great a beauty, and as great a jilt.

Plume. A jilt! pho! is she as great a whore?

Wor. No, no.

Plume. 'Tis ten thousand pities!—But who is she?—do I know her?

Wor. Very well.

Plume. That's impossible——I know no woman that will hold out a ten years' siege.

Wor. What think you of Melinda?

Plume. Melinda! why she began to capitulate this time twelvemonth, and offered to surrender upon honourable terms: and I advised you to propose a settlement of five hundred pounds a year to her, before I went last abroad.

Wor. I did, and she hearkened to it, desiring only one week to consider —when beyond her hopes the town was relieved, and I forced to turn the siege into a blockade.

Plume. Explain, explain.

Wor. My Lady Richly, her aunt in Flintshire, dies, and leaves her, at this critical time, twenty thousand pounds.

Plume. Oh, the devil! what a delicate woman was there spoiled! But, by the rules of war, now——Worthy, blockade was foolish—After such a convoy of provisions was entered the place, you could have no thought of reducing it by famine; you should have redoubled your attacks, taken the town by storm, or have died upon the breach.

Wor. I did make one general assault, but was so vigorously repulsed, that, despairing of ever gaining her for a mistress, I have altered my conduct, given my addresses the obsequious, and distant turn, and court her now for a wife.

Plume. So, as you grew obsequious, she grew haughty, and, because you approached her like a goddess, she used you like a dog.

Wor. Exactly.

Plume. 'Tis the way of them all——Come, Worthy, your obsequious and distant airs will never bring you together; you must not think to surmount her pride by your humility. Would you bring her to better thoughts of you, she must be reduced to a meaner opinion of herself. Let me see, the very first thing that I would do, should be, to lie with her chambermaid, and hire three or four wenches in the neighbourhood to report, that I had got them with child—Suppose we lampooned all the pretty women in town, and left her out; or, what if we made a ball, and forgot to invite her, with one or two of the ugliest.

Wor. These would be mortifications I must confess; but we live in such a precise, dull place, that we can have no balls, no lampoons, no——

Plume. What, no bastards! and so many recruiting officers in town! I thought 'twas a maxim among them, to leave as many recruits in the country as they carried out.

Wor. Nobody doubts your good will, noble captain, in serving your country; witness our friend Molly at the Castle; there have been tears in town about that business, captain.

Plume. I hope Sylvia has not heard of it.

Wor. Oh, sir, have you thought of her? I began to fancy you had forgot poor Sylvia.

Plume. Your affairs had quite put mine out of my head. 'Tis true, Sylvia and I had once agreed to go to bed together, could we have adjusted preliminaries; but she would have the wedding before consummation, and I was for consummation before the wedding: we could not agree.

Wor. But do you intend to marry upon no other conditions?

Plume. Your pardon, sir, I'll marry upon no condition at all—If I should, I am resolved never to bind myself down to a woman for my whole life, till I know whether I shall like her company for half an hour. Suppose I married a woman without a leg—such a thing might be, unless I examined the goods before-hand.—If people would but try one another's constitutions before they engaged, it would prevent all these elopements, divorces, and the devil knows what.

Wor. Nay, for that matter, the town did not stick to say that——

Plume. I hate country towns for that reason.—If your town has a dishonourable thought of Sylvia, it deserves to be burnt to the ground —I love Sylvia, I admire her frank, generous disposition—there's something in that girl more than woman—In short, were I once a general, I would marry her.

Wor. 'Faith, you have reason—for were you but a corporal, she would marry you—but my Melinda coquets it with every fellow she sees—I'll lay fifty pounds she makes love to you.

Plume. I'll lay you a hundred, that I return it if she does—Look ye, Worthy, I'll win her, and give her to you afterwards.

Wor. If you win her, you shall wear her, 'faith; I would not value the conquest, without the credit of the victory.

Enter KITE.

Kite. Captain, captain! a word in your ear.

Plume. You may speak out, here are none but friends.

Kite. You know, sir, that you sent me to comfort the good woman in the straw, Mrs. Molly—my wife, Mr. Worthy.

Wor. O ho! very well. I wish you joy, Mr. Kite.

Kite. Your worship very well may—for I have got both a wife and a child in half an hour—But as I was saying—you sent me to comfort Mrs. Molly—my wife, I mean—but what d'ye think, sir? she was better comforted before I came.

Plume. As how?

Kite. Why, sir, a footman in a blue livery had brought her ten guineas to buy her baby-clothes.

Plume. Who, in the name of wonder, could send them?

Kite. Nay, sir, I must whisper that—Mrs. Sylvia.

Plume. Sylvia! generous creature!

Wor. Sylvia! impossible!

Kite. Here are the guineas, sir—I took the gold as part of my wife's

10

portion. Nay, farther, sir, she sent word the child should be taken all imaginable care of, and that she intended to stand godmother. The same footman, as I was coming to you with this news, called after me, and told me, that his lady would speak to me—I went, and upon hearing that you were come to town, she gave me half a guinea for the news, and ordered me to tell you, that Justice Balance, her father, who is just come out of the country, would be glad to see you.

Plume. There's a girl for you, Worthy!—Is there any thing of woman in this? no, 'tis noble, generous, manly friendship. Show me another woman that would lose an inch of her prerogative that way, without tears, fits, and reproaches. The common jealousy of her sex, which is nothing but their avarice of pleasure, she despises, and can part with the lover, though she dies for the man—Come, Worthy—where's the best wine? for there I'll quarter.

Wor. At Horton's.

Plume. Let's away, then.—Mr. Kite, go to the lady, with my humble service, and tell her, I shall only refresh a little, and wait upon her.

Wor. Hold, Kite—have you seen the other recruiting captain?

Kite. No, sir; I'd have you to know I don't keep such company.

Plume. Another! who is he?

Wor. My rival, in the first place, and the most unaccountable fellow— but I'll tell you more as we go.

[*Exeunt.*

SCENE II.

An Apartment.

Melinda *and* Sylvia *meeting.*

Mel. Welcome to town, cousin Sylvia. [*Salute.*] I envied you your retreat in the country; for Shrewsbury, methinks, and all your heads of shires, are the most irregular places for living: here we have smoke, scandal, affectation, and pretension; in short, every thing to give the spleen— and nothing to divert it—then the air is intolerable.

Syl. Oh, madam! I have heard the town commended for its air.

Mel. But you don't consider, Sylvia, how long I have lived in it; for I

11

can assure you that to a lady the least nice in her constitution—no air can be good above half a year. Change of air I take to be the most agreeable of any variety in life.

Syl. As you say, cousin Melinda, there are several sorts of airs.

Mel. Psha! I talk only of the air we breathe, or more properly of that we taste—Have not you, Sylvia, found a vast difference in the taste of airs?

Syl. Pray, cousin, are not vapours a sort of air? Taste air! you might as well tell me I may feed upon air! but pr'ythee, my dear Melinda! don't put on such an air to me. Your education and mine were just the same, and I remember the time when we never troubled our heads about air, but when the sharp air from the Welsh mountains made our fingers ache in a cold morning, at the boarding-school.

Mel. Our education, cousin, was the same, but our temperaments had nothing alike; you have the constitution of an horse.

Syl. So far as to be troubled neither with spleen, cholic, nor vapours. I need no salts for my stomach, no hartshorn for my head, nor wash for my complexion; I can gallop all the morning after the hunting-horn, and all the evening after a fiddle. In short, I can do every thing with my father, but drink and shoot flying; and I am sure I can do every thing my mother could, were I put to the trial.

Mel. You are in a fair way of being put to't, for I am told your captain is come to town.

Syl. Ay, Melinda, he is come, and I'll take care he shan't go without a companion.

Mel. You are certainly mad, cousin!

Syl. "And there's a pleasure in being mad,
Which none but madmen know".

Mel. Thou poor romantic Quixote!—hast thou the vanity to imagine that a young sprightly officer, that rambles o'er half the globe in half a year, can confine his thoughts to the little daughter of a country justice, in an obscure part of the world?

Syl. Psha! what care I for his thoughts; I should not like a man with confined thoughts; it shows a narrowness of soul. In short, Melinda, I think a petticoat a mighty simple thing, and I am heartily tired of my sex.

Mel. That is, you are tired of an appendix to our sex, that you can't so handsomely get rid of in petticoats as if you were in breeches.—O'my conscience, Sylvia, hadst thou been a man, thou hadst been the greatest rake in Christendom.

Syl. I should have endeavoured to know the world, which a man can never do thoroughly without half a hundred friendships, and as many amours. But now I think on't, how stands your affair with Mr. Worthy?

Mel. He's my aversion.

Syl. Vapours!

Mel. What do you say, madam?

Syl. I say, that you should not use that honest fellow so inhumanly: he's a gentleman of parts and fortune, and besides that, he's my Plume's friend; and by all that's sacred, if you don't use him better, I shall expect satisfaction.

Mel. Satisfaction! you begin to fancy yourself in breeches in good earnest—But, to be plain with you, I like Worthy the worse for being so intimate with your captain; for I take him to be a loose, idle, unmannerly coxcomb.

Syl. Oh, Madam! you never saw him, perhaps, since you were mistress of twenty thousand pounds: you only knew him when you were capitulating with Worthy for a settlement, which perhaps might encourage him to be a little loose and unmannerly with you.

Mel. What do you mean, madam?

Syl. My meaning needs no interpretation, madam.

Mel. Better it had, madam; for methinks you are too plain.

Syl. If you mean the plainness of my person, I think your ladyship's as plain as me to the full.

Mel. Were I sure of that, I would be glad to take up with a rakehelly officer, as you do.

Syl. Again! lookye, madam, you are in your own house.

Mel. And if you had kept in yours, I should have excused you.

Syl. Don't be troubled, madam; I shan't desire to have my visit returned.

Mel. The sooner, therefore, you make an end of this, the better.

Syl. I am easily persuaded to follow my inclinations; and so, madam, your humble servant.

[*Exit.*

Mel. Saucy thing!

Enter LUCY.

Lucy. What's the matter, madam?

Mel. Did not you see the proud nothing, how she swelled upon the arrival of her fellow?

Lucy. Her fellow has not been long enough arrived, to occasion any great swelling, madam; I don't believe she has seen him yet.

Mel. Nor shan't, if I can help it.—Let me see—I have it; bring me pen and ink—Hold, I'll go write in my closet.

Lucy. An answer to this letter, I hope, madam?

[*Presents a Letter.*

Mel. Who sent it?

Lucy. Your captain, madam.

Mel. He's a fool, and I'm tired of him: send it back unopened.

Lucy. The messenger's gone, madam.

Mel. Then how should I send an answer? Call him back immediately, while I go write.

[*Exeunt.*

ACT II.

SCENE I.

An Apartment.

Enter JUSTICE BALANCE *and* PLUME.

Bal. Lookye, captain, give us but blood for our money, and you shan't want men. Ad's my life, captain, get us but another marshal of France, and I'll go myself for a soldier.

Plume. Pray, Mr. Balance, how does your fair daughter?

Bal. Ah, captain! what is my daughter to a marshal of France? we're upon a nobler subject; I want to have a particular description of the last battle.

Plume. The battle, sir, was a very pretty battle as any one should desire to see; but we were all so intent upon victory, that we never minded the battle: all that I know of the matter is, our general commanded us to beat the French, and we did so; and, if he pleases but to say the word, we'll do it again. But pray, sir, how does Mrs. Sylvia?

Bal. Still upon Sylvia! for shame, captain! you are engaged already—wedded to the war: victory is your mistress, and 'tis below a soldier to think of any other.

Plume. As a mistress, I confess—but as a friend, Mr. Balance——

Bal. Come, come, captain, never mince the matter; would not you seduce my daughter, if you could?

Plume. How, sir? I hope she is not to be seduced.

Bal. 'Faith, but she is, sir; and any woman in England of her age and complexion, by your youth and vigour. Lookye, captain, once I was young, and once an officer, as you are, and I can guess at your thoughts now by what mine were then; and I remember very well that I would have given one of my legs to have deluded the daughter of an old country gentleman like me, as I was then like you.

Plume. But, sir, was that country gentleman your friend and benefactor?

Bal. Not much of that.

Plume. There the comparison breaks: the favours, sir, that——

15

Bal. Pho, pho! I hate set speeches: if I have done you any service, captain, it was to please myself. I love thee, and if I could part with my girl, you should have her as soon as any young fellow I know; but I hope you have more honour than to quit the service, and she more prudence than to follow the camp: but she's at her own disposal; she has five thousand pounds in her pocket, and so—Sylvia, Sylvia!

[*Calls.*

Enter SYLVIA.

Syl. There are some letters, sir, come by the post from London; I left them upon the table in your closet.

Bal. And here is a gentleman from Germany.—[*Presents* PLUME *to her.*] Captain, you'll excuse me; I'll go read my letters, and wait on you.

[*Exit.*

Syl. Sir, you are welcome to England.

Plume. You are indebted to me a welcome, madam, since the hopes of receiving it from this fair hand was the principal cause of my seeing England.

Syl. I have often heard that soldiers were sincere; may I venture to believe public report?

Plume. You may, when 'tis backed by private insurance; for I swear, madam, by the honour of my profession, that whatever dangers I went upon, it was with the hope of making myself more worthy of your esteem; and if ever I had thoughts of preserving my life, 'twas for the pleasure of dying at your feet.

Syl. Well, well, you shall die at my feet, or where you will; but you know, sir, there is a certain will and testament to be made beforehand.

Plume. My will, madam, is made already, and there it is; and if you please to open that parchment, which was drawn the evening before the battle of Hockstet, you will find whom I left my heir.

Syl. *Mrs. Sylvia Balance.* [*Opens the Will, and reads.*] Well, captain, this is a handsome and substantial compliment; but I can assure you I am much better pleased with the bare knowledge of your intention, than I should have been in the possession of your legacy: but, methinks, sir, you should have left something to your little boy at the Castle.

16

Plume. That's home. [*Aside.*] My little boy! lack-a-day, madam! that alone may convince you 'twas none of mine: why, the girl, madam, is my serjeant's wife, and so the poor creature gave out that I was the father, in hopes that my friends might support her in case of necessity. —That was all, madam—my boy! no, no, no!

Enter a SERVANT.

Serv. Madam, my master has received some ill news from London, and desires to speak with you immediately; and he begs the captain's pardon, that he can't wait on him, as he promised.

Plume. Ill news! Heavens avert it! nothing could touch me nearer than to see that generous, worthy gentleman afflicted. I'll leave you to comfort him; and be assured that if my life and fortune can be any way serviceable to the father of my Sylvia, he shall freely command both.

Syl. The necessity must be very pressing that would engage me to endanger either.

[*Exeunt severally.*

SCENE II.

Another Apartment.

Enter BALANCE *and* SYLVIA.

Syl. Whilst there is life there is hope, sir; perhaps my brother may recover.

Bal. We have but little reason to expect it; the doctor acquaints me here, that before this comes to my hands he fears I shall have no son.— Poor Owen! but the decree is just; I was pleased with the death of my father, because he left me an estate; and now I am punished with the loss of an heir to inherit mine. I must now look upon you as the only hopes of my family; and I expect that the augmentation of your fortune will give you fresh thoughts and new prospects.

Syl. My desire in being punctual in my obedience, requires that you would be plain in your commands, sir.

Bal. The death of your brother makes you sole heiress to my estate, which you know is about three thousand pounds a year: this fortune gives you a fair claim to quality and a title: you must set a just value upon yourself, and, in plain terms, think no more of Captain Plume.

17

Syl. You have often commended the gentleman, sir.

Bal. And I do so still; he's a very pretty fellow; but though I liked him well enough for a bare son-in-law, I don't approve of him for an heir to my estate and family; five thousand pounds indeed I might trust in his hands, and it might do the young fellow a kindness; but—od's my life! three thousand pounds a year would ruin him, quite turn his brain—A captain of foot worth three thousand pounds a year! 'tis a prodigy in nature!

Enter a SERVANT.

Serv. Sir, here's one with a letter below for your worship, but he will deliver it into no hands but your own.

Bal. Come, show me the messenger.

[*Exit with* SERVANT.

Syl. Make the dispute between love and duty, and I am prince Prettyman exactly.—If my brother dies, ah, poor brother! if he lives, ah, poor sister! It is bad both ways, I'll try it again—Follow my own inclinations, and break my father's heart; or obey his commands, and break my own? Worse and worse.—Suppose I take it thus: A moderate fortune, a pretty fellow, and a pad; or a fine estate, a coach and six, and an ass.—That will never do neither.

Enter BALANCE *and a* SERVANT.

Bal. Put four horses to the coach. [*To a* SERVANT, *who goes out.*] Ho, Sylvia!

Syl. Sir.

Bal. How old were you when your mother died?

Syl. So young that I don't remember I ever had one; and you have been so careful, so indulgent to me since, that indeed I never wanted one.

Bal. Have I ever denied you any thing you asked of me?

Syl. Never, that I remember.

Bal. Then, Sylvia, I must beg that once in your life you would grant me a favour.

Syl. Why should you question it, sir?

18

Bal. I don't; but I would rather counsel than command. I don't propose this with the authority of a parent, but as the advice of your friend, that you would take the coach this moment, and go into the country.

Syl. Does this advice, sir, proceed from the contents of the letter you received just now?

Bal. No matter; I will be with you in three or four days, and then give my reasons: but before you go, I expect you will make me one solemn promise.

Syl. Propose the thing, sir.

Bal. That you will never dispose of yourself to any man without my consent.

Syl. I promise.

Bal. Very well; and to be even with you, I promise I never will dispose of you without your own consent: and so, Sylvia, the coach is ready. Farewell. [*Leads her to the Door, and returns.*] Now, she's gone, I'll examine the contents of this letter a little nearer.

[*Reads.*

Sir,

My intimacy with Mr. Worthy has drawn a secret from him, that he had from his friend Captain Plume; and my friendship and relation to your family oblige me to give you timely notice of it. The captain has dishonourable designs upon my cousin Sylvia. Evils of this nature are more easily prevented than amended; and that you would immediately send my cousin into the country, is the advice of,

Sir, your humble servant,

Melinda.

Why, the devil's in the young fellows of this age; they are ten times worse than they were in my time: had he made my daughter a whore, and forswore it, like a gentleman, I could almost have pardoned it; but to tell tales beforehand is monstrous.—Hang it! I can fetch down a woodcock or a snipe, and why not a hat and cockade? I have a case of good pistols, and have a good mind to try.

Enter WORTHY.

Worthy, your servant.

Wor. I'm sorry, sir, to be the messenger of ill news.

Bal. I apprehend it, sir; you have heard that my son Owen is past recovery.

Wor. My letters say he's dead, sir.

Bal. He's happy, and I am satisfied: the stroke of Heaven I can bear; but injuries from men, Mr. Worthy, are not so easily supported.

Wor. I hope, sir, you are under no apprehensions of wrong from any body.

Bal. You know I ought to be.

Wor. You wrong my honour, in believing I could know any thing to your prejudice, without resenting it as much as you should.

Bal. This letter, sir, which I tear in pieces, to conceal the person that sent it, informs me that Plume has a design upon Sylvia, and that you are privy to it.

Wor. Nay, then, sir, I must do myself justice, and endeavour to find out the author. [*Takes up a Bit.*]—Sir, I know the hand, and if you refuse to discover the contents, Melinda shall tell me.

[*Going.*

Bal. Hold, sir; the contents I have told you already; only with this circumstance—that her intimacy with Mr. Worthy had drawn the secret from him.

Wor. Her intimacy with me! Dear sir! let me pick up the pieces of this letter, 'twill give me such a power over her pride to have her own an intimacy under her hand.—This was the luckiest accident! [*Gathering up the Letter.*] The aspersion, sir, was nothing but malice; the effect of a little quarrel between her and Mrs. Sylvia.

Bal. Are you sure of that, sir?

Wor. Her maid gave me the history of part of the battle just now, as she overheard it: but I hope, sir, your daughter has suffered nothing upon the account.

20

Bal. No, no, poor girl! she's so afflicted with the news of her brother's death, that, to avoid company, she begged leave to go into the country.

Wor. And is she gone?

Bal. I could not refuse her, she was so pressing; the coach went from the door the minute before you came.

Wor. So pressing to be gone, sir?—I find her fortune will give her the same airs with Melinda, and then Plume and I may laugh at one another.

Bal. Like enough; women are as subject to pride as men are; and why mayn't great women as well as great men forget their old acquaintance? But come, where's this young fellow? I love him so well, it would break the heart of me to think him a rascal.—I am glad my daughter's gone fairly off though.—[*Aside.*] Where does the captain quarter?

Wor. At Horton's; I am to meet him there two hours hence, and we should be glad of your company.

Bal. Your pardon, dear Worthy! I must allow a day or two to the death of my son. The decorum of mourning is what we owe the world, because they pay it to us; afterwards I'm yours over a bottle, or how you will.

Wor. Sir, I'm your humble servant.

[*Exeunt apart.*

SCENE III.

The Street.

Enter Kite, *with* Costar Pearmain *in one Hand, and* Thomas Appletree *in the other, drunk.*

Kite *sings.*

Our 'prentice Tom may now refuse
To wipe his scoundrel master's shoes,
For now he's free to sing and play
Over the hills and far away.
Over, &c.

[*The Mob sing the Chorus.*

We shall lead more happy lives
By getting rid of brats and wives,
That scold and brawl both night and day,
Over the hills and far away.
Over, &c.

Kite. Hey, boys! thus we soldiers live! drink, sing, dance, play;—we live, as one should say—we live—'tis impossible to tell how we live—we are all princes—why, why you are a king—you are an emperor, and I'm a prince—now, an't we?

Tho. No serjeant, I'll be no emperor.

Kite. No!

Tho. I'll be a justice of peace.

Kite. A justice of peace, man!

Tho. Ay, wauns will I; for since this pressing act, they are greater than any emperor under the sun.

Kite. Done; you are a justice of peace, and you are a king, and I am a duke, and a rum duke, an't I?

Cost. I'll be a queen.

Kite. A queen.

Cost. Ay, of England, that's greater than any king of them all.

Kite. Bravely said, 'faith! huzza for the queen. [*Huzza.*] But harkye, you Mr. Justice, and you Mr. Queen, did you ever see the king's picture?

Both. No! no! no!

Kite. I wonder at that; I have two of them set in gold, and as like his majesty, God bless the mark! see here, they are set in gold.

[*Takes two broad pieces out of his pocket; presents one to each.*

Tho. The wonderful works of nature! [*Looking at it.*

What's this written about? here's a posy, I believe.—Ca-ro-lus!—what's that, serjeant?

22

Kite. O! Carolus! why, Carolus is Latin for King George; that's all.

Cost. Tis a fine thing to be a scollard.—Serjeant, will you part with this? I'll buy it on you, if it come within the compass of a crown.

Kite. A crown! never talk of buying; 'tis the same thing among friends, you know; I'll present them to ye both: you shall give me as good a thing. Put them up, and remember your old friend when I am over the hills and far away.

[*They sing, and put up the Money.*

Enter PLUME, *singing.*

Over the hills and over the main,
To Flanders, Portugal, or Spain;
The king commands and we'll obey,
Over the hills and far away.

Come on my men of mirth, away with it; I'll make one among ye. Who are these hearty lads?

Kite. Off with your hats; 'ounds! off with your hats: this is the captain, the captain.

Tho. We have seen captains afore now, mun.

Cost. Ay, and lieutenant-captains too. 'Sflesh! I'll keep on my nab.

Tho. And I'se scarcely d'off mine for any captain in England. My vether's a freeholder.

Plume. Who are those jolly lads, serjeant?

Kite. A couple of honest brave fellows that are willing to serve the king: I have entertained them just now as volunteers, under your honour's command.

Plume. And good entertainment they shall have: volunteers are the men I want; those are the men fit to make soldiers, captains, generals.

Cost. Wounds, Tummas, what's this! are you listed?

Tho. Flesh! not I: are you, Costar?

Cost. Wounds! not I.

23

Kite. What! not listed? ha! ha! ha! a very good jest, i'faith.

Cost. Come, Tummus, we'll go home.

Tho. Ay, ay, come.

Kite. Home! for shame, gentlemen; behave yourselves better before your captain. Dear Tummas, honest Costar!

Tho. No, no! we'll be gone.

Kite. Nay, then, I command you to stay: I place you both centinels in this place for two hours, to watch the motion of St. Mary's clock you, and you the motion of St. Chad's; and he, that dares stir from his post till he be relieved, shall have my sword in his guts the next minute.

Plume. What's the matter, serjeant? I'm afraid you are too rough with these gentlemen.

Kite. I'm too mild, sir; they disobey command, sir; and one of them should be shot, for an example to the other.

Cost. Shot! Tummas?

Plume. Come, gentlemen, what's the matter?

Tho. We don't know; the noble serjeant is pleas'd to be in a passion, sir; but——

Kite. They disobey command; they deny their being listed.

Tho. Nay, serjeant, we don't downright deny it, neither; that we dare not do, for fear of being shot; but we humbly conceive, in a civil way, and begging your worship's pardon, that we may go home.

Plume. That's easily known. Have either of you received any of the king's money?

Cost. Not a brass farthing, sir.

Kite. They have each of them received one-and-twenty shillings, and 'tis now in their pockets.

Cost. Wounds! if I have a penny in my pocket but a bent sixpence, I'll be content to be listed and shot into the bargain.

Tho. And I: look ye here, sir.

Cost. Nothing but the king's picture, that the serjeant gave me just now.

Kite. See there, a guinea, one and twenty shillings; t'other has the fellow on't.

Plume. The case is plain, gentlemen: the goods are found upon you: those pieces of gold are worth one-and-twenty shillings each.

Cost. So it seems that Carolus is one-and-twenty shillings in Latin.

Tho. 'Tis the same thing in Greek, for we are listed.

Cost. Flesh; but we an't, Tummus: I desire to be carried before the mayor, captain.

[CAPTAIN *and* SERJEANT *whisper the while.*

Plume. 'Twill never do, Kite—your damned tricks will ruin me at last—I won't lose the fellows, though, if I can help it.—Well, gentlemen, there must be some trick in this; my serjeant offers to take his oath that you are fairly listed.

Tho. Why, captain, we know that you soldiers have more liberty of conscience than other folks; but for me or neighbour Costar here to take such an oath, 'twould be downright perjuration.

Plume. Lookye, rascal, you villain! If I find that you have imposed upon these two honest fellows, I'll trample you to death, you dog—Come, how was't?

Tho. Nay, then we'll speak. Your serjeant, as you say, is a rogue, an't like your worship, begging your worship's pardon—and—

Cost. Nay, Tummus, let me speak, you know I can read.——And so, sir, he gave us those two pieces of money for pictures of the king, by way of a present.

Plume. How? by way of a present! the son of a whore! I'll teach him to abuse honest fellows like you!—scoundrel! rogue! villain!

[*Beats off the Serjeant, and follows.*

Both. O brave noble captain! huzza! A brave captain, 'faith!

Cost. Now, Tummas, Carolus is Latin for a beating. This is the bravest captain I ever saw—Wounds! I've a month's mind to go with him.

25

Enter PLUME.

Plume. A dog, to abuse two such honest fellows as you.—Lookye, gentlemen, I love a pretty fellow; I come among you as an officer to list soldiers, not as a kidnapper to steal slaves.

Cost. Mind that, Tummas.

Plume. I desire no man to go with me but as I went myself; I went a volunteer, as you or you may do; for a little time carried a musket, and now I command a company.

Tho. Mind that, Costar. A sweet gentleman!

Plume. Tis true, gentlemen, I might take an advantage of you; the king's money was in your pockets—my serjeant was ready to take his oath you were listed; but I scorn to do a base thing; you are both of you at your liberty.

Cost. Thank you, noble captain———Icod! I can't find in my heart to leave him, he talks so finely.

Tho. Ay, Costar, would he always hold in this mind.

Plume. Come, my lads, one thing more I'll tell you: you're both young tight fellows, and the army is the place to make you men for ever: every man has his lot, and you have yours: what think you of a purse of French gold out of a monsieur's pocket, after you have dashed out his brains with the but end of your firelock, eh?

Cost. Wauns! I'll have it. Captain—give me a shilling; I'll follow you to the end of the world.

Tho. Nay, dear Costar! do'na: be advis'd.

Plume. Here, my hero, here are two guineas for thee, as earnest of what I'll do farther for thee.

Tho. Do'na take it; do'na, dear Costar.

[*Cries, and pulls back his Arm.*

Cost. I wull—I wull—Waunds! my mind gives me that I shall be a captain myself—I take your money, sir, and now I am a gentleman.

Plume. Give me thy hand; and now you and I will travel the world o'er, and command it wherever we tread.—Bring your friend with you, if you can. [*Aside.*

Cost. Well, Tummas, must we part?

Tho. No, Costar, I cannot leave thee.—Come, captain, I'll e'en go along too; and if you have two honester simpler lads in your company than we two have been, I'll say no more.

Plume. Here, my lad. [*Gives him Money.*] Now, your name?

Tho. Tummas Appletree.

Plume. And yours?

Cost. Costar Pearmain.

Plume. Well said, Costar! Born where?

Tho. Both in Herefordshire.

Plume. Very well. Courage, my lads. Now we'll

> *Sings.*   *Over the hills, and far away.*
>   *Courage, boys, it's one to ten*
>   *But we return all gentlemen;*
>   *While conq'ring colours we display,*
>   *Over the hills, and far away.*

Kite, take care of them.

Enter K<small>ITE</small>.

Kite. An't you a couple of pretty fellows, now! Here, you have complained to the captain; I am to be turned out, and one of you will be serjeant. Which of you is to have my halberd?

Both Rec. I.

Kite. So you shall—in your guts.—March, you sons of whores!

[Beats them off.

ACT III.

SCENE I.

The Market Place.

Enter PLUME *and* WORTHY.

Wor. I cannot forbear admiring the equality of our fortunes: we love two ladies, they meet us half way, and just as we were upon the point of leaping into their arms, fortune drops in their laps, pride possesses their hearts, a maggot fills their heads, madness takes them by the tails; they snort, kick up their heels, and away they run.

Plume. And leave us here to mourn upon the shore—a couple of poor melancholy monsters. What shall we do?

Wor. I have a trick for mine; the letter, you know, and the fortune-teller.

Plume. And I have a trick for mine.

Wor. What is't?

Plume. I'll never think of her again.

Wor. No!

Plume. No; I think myself above administering to the pride of any woman, were she worth twelve thousand a-year; and I ha'n't the vanity to believe I shall gain a lady worth twelve hundred. The generous, goodnatured Sylvia, in her smock, I admire; but the haughty and scornful Sylvia, with her fortune, I despise.—What! sneak out of town, and not so much as a word, a line, a compliment!—'Sdeath! how far off does she live? I'll go and break her windows.

Wor. Ha! ha! ha! ay, and the window-bars too, to come at her. Come, come, friend, no more of your rough military airs.

Enter KITE.

Kite. Captain! captain! Sir, look yonder; she's a-coming this way. 'Tis the prettiest, cleanest, little tit!

Plume. Now, Worthy, to show you how much I'm in love—here she comes. But, Kite, what is that great country fellow with her?

Kite. I can't tell, sir.

Enter Rose, *followed by her Brother* Bullock, *with Chickens on her Arm, in a Basket.*

Rose. Buy chickens, young and tender chickens, young and tender chickens.

Plume. Here, you chickens.

Rose. Who calls?

Plume. Come hither, pretty maid.

Rose. Will you please to buy, sir?

Wor. Yes, child, we'll both buy.

Plume. Nay, Worthy, that's not fair; market for yourself—Come, child, I'll buy all you have.

Rose. Then all I have is at your service.

[*Courtesies.*

Wor. Then must I shift for myself, I find.

[*Exit.*

Plume. Let me see; young and tender, you say.

[*Chucks her under the Chin.*

Rose. As ever you tasted in your life, sir.

Plume. Come, I must examine your basket to the bottom, my dear!

Rose. Nay, for that matter, put in your hand; feel, sir; I warrant my ware is as good as any in the market.

Plume. And I'll buy it all, child, were it ten times more.

Rose. Sir, I can furnish you.

Plume. Come, then, we won't quarrel about the price; they're fine birds. —Pray, what's your name, pretty creature!

Rose. Rose, sir. My father is a farmer within three short miles o' the town: we keep this market; I sell chickens, eggs, and butter, and my brother Bullock there sells corn.

30

Bul. Come, sister, haste—we shall be late home.

[*Whistles about the Stage.*

Plume. Kite! [*Tips him the wink, he returns it.*] Pretty Mrs. Rose—you have—let me see—how many?

Rose. A dozen, sir, and they are richly worth a crown.

Bul. Come, Rouse; I sold fifty strake of barley to-day in half this time; but you will higgle and higgle for a penny more than the commodity is worth.

Rose. What's that to you, oaf? I can make as much out of a groat as you can out of fourpence, I'm sure—The gentleman bids fair, and when I meet with a chapman, I know how to make the best of him—And so, sir, I say for a crown-piece the bargain's yours.

Plume. Here's a guinea, my dear!

Rose. I can't change your money, sir.

Plume. Indeed, indeed, but you can—my lodging is hard by, chicken! and we'll make change there.

[*Goes off, she follows him.*

Kite. So, sir, as I was telling you, I have seen one of these hussars eat up a ravelin for his breakfast, and afterwards pick his teeth with a palisado.

Bul. Ay, you soldiers see very strange things; but pray, sir, what is a rabelin?

Kite. Why, 'tis like a modern minc'd pie, but the crust is confounded hard, and the plums are somewhat hard of digestion.

Bul. Then your palisado, pray what may he be? Come, Rouse, pray ha' done.

Kite. Your palisado is a pretty sort of bodkin, about the thickness of my leg.

Bul. That's a fib, I believe. [*Aside.*] Eh! where's Rouse? Rouse, Rouse! 'Sflesh! where's Rouse gone?

Kite. She's gone with the captain.

Bul. The captain! wauns! there's no pressing of women, sure.

31

Kite. But there is, sure.

Bul. If the captain should press Rouse, I should be ruined——Which way went she? Oh! the devil take your rabelins and palisadoes!

[*Exit.*

Kite. You shall be better acquainted with them, honest Bullock, or I shall miss of my aim.

Enter WORTHY.

Wor. Why thou art the most useful fellow in nature to your captain, admirable in your way I find.

Kite. Yes, sir, I understand my business, I will say it.

Wor. How came you so qualified?

Kite. You must know, sir, I was born a gipsy, and bred among that crew till I was ten years old; there I learned canting and lying: I was bought from my mother Cleopatra by a certain nobleman for three pistoles, there I learned impudence and pimping: I was turned off for wearing my lord's linen, and drinking my lady's ratafia, and turned bailiff's follower; there I learned bullying and swearing: I at last got into the army; and there I learned whoring and drinking—so that if your worship pleases to cast up the whole sum, viz. canting, lying, impudence, pimping, bullying, swearing, whoring, drinking, and a halberd, you will find the sum total amount to a Recruiting Serjeant.

Wor. And pray what induced you to turn soldier?

Kite. Hunger and ambition. But here comes Justice Balance.

Enter BALANCE *and* BULLOCK.

Bal. Here you, serjeant, where's your captain? here's a poor foolish fellow comes clamouring to me with a complaint that your captain has pressed his sister. Do you know any thing of this matter, Worthy?

Wor. Ha! ha! ha! I know his sister is gone with Plume to his lodging, to sell him some chickens.

Bal. Is that all? the fellow's a fool.

Bul. I know that, an't like your worship; but if your worship pleases to grant me a warrant to bring her before your worship, for fear of the worst.

Bal. Thou'rt mad, fellow; thy sister's safe enough.

Kite. I hope so too. [*Aside.*

Wor. Hast thou no more sense, fellow, than to believe that the captain can list women?

Bul. I know not whether they list them, or what they do with them, but I'm sure they carry as many women as men with them out of the country.

Bal. But how came you not to go along with your sister?

Bul. Lord, sir, I thought no more of her going than I do of the day I shall die: but this gentleman here, not suspecting any hurt neither, I believe—you thought no harm, friend, did you?

Kite. Lack-a-day, sir, not I——only that I believe I shall marry her to-morrow.

Bal. I begin to smell powder. Well, friend, but what did that gentleman with you?

Bul. Why, sir, he entertained me with a fine story of a great sea-fight between the Hungarians, I think it was, and the wild Irish.

Kite. And so, sir, while we were in the heat of battle—the captain carried off the baggage.

Bal. Serjeant, go along with this fellow to your captain, give him my humble service, and desire him to discharge the wench, though he has listed her.

Bul. Ay, and if she ben't free for that, he shall have another man in her place.

Kite. Come, honest friend, you shall go to my quarters instead of the captain's. [*Aside.*

[*Exeunt* KITE *and* BULLOCK.

Bal. We must get this mad captain his complement of men, and send him packing, else he'll overrun the country.

Wor. You see, sir, how little he values your daughter's disdain.

Bal. I like him the better: I was just such another fellow at his age: But how goes your affair with Melinda?

Wor. Very slowly. My mistress has got a captain too, but such a captain! —as I live, yonder he comes!

Bal. Who, that bluff fellow in the sash? I don't know him.

Wor. But I engage he knows you and every body at first sight: his impudence were a prodigy, were not his ignorance proportionable; he has the most universal acquaintance of any man living, for he won't be alone, and nobody will keep him company twice: then he's a Cæsar among the women, *veni, vidi, vici,* that's all. If he has but talked with the maid, he swears he has lain with the mistress: but the most surprising part of his character is his memory, which is the most prodigious and the most trifling in the world.

Bal. I have known another acquire so much by travel as to tell you the names of most places in Europe, with their distances of miles, leagues, or hours, as punctually as a postboy; but for any thing else as ignorant as the horse that carries the mail.

Wor. This is your man, sir, add but the traveller's privilege of lying, and even that he abuses: this is the picture, behold the life.

Enter BRAZEN.

Brazen. Mr. Worthy, I'm your servant, and so forth—Harkye, my dear!

Wor. Whispering, sir, before company, is not manners, and when nobody's by 'tis foolish.

Brazen. Company! *mort de ma vie!* I beg the gentleman's pardon—who is he?

Wor. Ask him.

Brazen. So I will. My dear! I am your servant, and so forth—Your name, my dear?

Bal. Very laconic, sir.

Brazen. Laconic! a very good name truly. I have known several of the Laconics abroad. Poor Jack Laconic! he was killed at the battle of Landen. I remember that he had a blue ribband in his hat that very day, and after he fell, we found a piece of neat's tongue in his pocket.

Bal. Pray, sir, did the French attack us, or we them, at Landen?

Brazen. The French attack us! No, sir, we attacked them on the——I have reason to remember the time, for I had two-and-twenty horses killed under me that day.

Wor. Then, sir, you must have rid mighty hard.

Bal. Or, perhaps, sir, like my countrymen, you rid upon half a dozen horses at once.

Brazen. What do ye mean, gentlemen? I tell you they were killed, all torn to pieces by cannon-shot, except six I staked to death upon the enemy's *cheveaux de frise*.

Bal. Noble captain! may I crave your name?

Brazen. Brazen, at your service.

Bal. Oh, Brazen! a very good name. I have known several of the Brazens abroad.

Wor. Do you know one Captain Plume, sir?

Brazen. Is he any thing related to Frank Plume in Northamptonshire? —Honest Frank! many, many a dry bottle have we cracked hand to fist. You must have known his brother Charles, that was concerned in the India company; he married the daughter of Old Tonguepad, the master in Chancery, a very pretty woman, only she quinted a little; she died in child-bed of her first child, but the child survived: 'twas a daughter, but whether it was called Margaret or Margery, upon my soul, I can't remember. [*Looking on his Watch.*] But, gentlemen, I must meet a lady, a twenty thousand pounder, presently, upon the walk by the water— Worthy, your servant; Laconic, yours.

[*Exit.*

Bal. If you can have so mean an opinion of Melinda, as to be jealous of this fellow, I think she ought to give you cause to be so.

Wor. I don't think she encourages him so much for gaining herself a lover, as to set up a rival. Were there any credit to be given to his words, I should believe Melinda had made him this assignation. I must go see, sir, you'll pardon me.

[*Exit.*

Bal. Ay, ay, sir, you're a man of business—But what have we got here?

Enter ROSE, *singing.*

Rose. And I shall be a lady, a captain's lady, and ride single, upon a white horse with a star, upon a velvet side-saddle; and I shall go to London, and see the tombs, and the lions, and the king and queen. Sir, an please your worship, I have often seen your worship ride through our grounds a-hunting, begging your worship's pardon. Pray, what may this lace be worth a-yard? [*Showing some Lace.*

Bal. Right Mecklin, by this light! Where did you get this lace, child?

Rose. No matter for that, sir; I came honestly by it.

Bal. I question it much. [*Aside.*

Rose. And see here, sir, a fine Turkey-shell snuff-box, and fine mangere: see here. [*Takes Snuff affectedly.*] The captain learned me how to take it with an air.

Bal. Oh ho! the captain! now the murder's out. And so the captain taught you to take it with an air?

Rose. Yes; and give it with an air too. Will your worship please to taste my snuff? [*Offers the Box affectedly.*

Bal. You are a very apt scholar, pretty maid! And pray, what did you give the captain for these fine things?

Rose. He's to have my brother for a soldier, and two or three sweethearts I have in the country; they shall all go with the captain. Oh! he's the finest man, and the humblest withal! Would you believe it, sir? he carried me up with him to his own chamber, with as much fam-mam-mil-yararality, as if I had been the best lady in the land.

Bal. Oh! he's a mighty familiar gentleman as can be.

Enter PLUME, *singing.*

Plume.   *But it is not so*
          With those that go
          Thro' frost and snow——
          Most apropos,
          My maid with the milking pail.

[*Takes hold of* ROSE.

36

How, the justice! then I'm arraigned, condemned and executed.

Bal. Oh, my noble captain!

Rose. And my noble captain, too, sir.

Plume. 'Sdeath! child, are you mad?—Mr. Balance, I am so full of business about my recruits, that I ha'n't a moment's time to——I have just now three or four people to——

Bal. Nay, captain, I must speak to you—

Rose. And so must I too, captain.

Plume. Any other time, sir—I cannot, for my life, sir—

Bal. Pray, sir——

Plume. Twenty thousand things—I would—but—now, sir, pray—Devil take me—I cannot—I must— [*Breaks away.*

Bal. Nay, I'll follow you.

[*Exit.*

Rose. And I too.

[*Exit.*

SCENE II.

The Walk by the Severn Side.

Enter MELINDA *and her Maid* LUCY.

Mel. And pray was it a ring, or buckle, or pendants, or knots; or in what shape was the almighty gold transformed, that has bribed you so much in his favour?

Lucy. Indeed, madam, the last bribe I had from the captain, was only a small piece of Flanders' lace, for a cap.

Mel. Ay, Flanders' lace is a constant present from officers to their women. They every year bring over a cargo of lace, to cheat the king of his duty, and his subjects of their honesty.

Lucy. They only barter one sort of prohibited goods for another, madam.

Mel. Has any of them been bartering with you, Mrs. Pert, that you talk so like a trader?

Lucy. One would imagine, madam, by your concern for Worthy's absence, that you should use him better when he's with you.

Mel. Who told you, pray, that I was concerned for his absence? I'm only vexed that I have had nothing said to me these two days: as one may love the treason and hate the traitor. Oh! here comes another captain, and a rogue that has the confidence to make love to me; but indeed, I don't wonder at that, when he has the assurance to fancy himself a fine gentleman.

Lucy. If he should speak o' th' assignation I should be ruined! [*Aside.*

Enter BRAZEN.

Brazen. True to the touch, 'faith! [*Aside.*] Madam, I am your humble servant, and all that, madam. A fine river, this same Severn—Do you love fishing, madam?

Mel. 'Tis a pretty melancholy amusement for lovers.

Brazen. I'll go and buy hooks and lines presently; for you must know, madam, that I have served in Flanders against the French, in Hungary against the Turks, and in Tangier against the Moors, and I was never so much in love before; and split me, madam, in all the campaigns I ever made, I have not seen so fine a woman as your ladyship.

Mel. And from all the men I ever saw, I never had so fine a compliment: but you soldiers are the best bred men, that we must allow.

Brazen. Some of us, madam; but there are brutes among us too, very sad brutes; for my own part, I have always had the good luck to prove agreeable. I have had very considerable offers, madam—I might have married a German princess, worth fifty thousand crowns a-year, but her stove disgusted me. The daughter of a Turkish bashaw fell in love with me, too, when I was a prisoner among the Infidels; she offered to rob her father of his treasure, and make her escape with me; but I don't know how, my time was not come: hanging and marriage, you know, go by destiny: Fate has reserved me for a Shropshire lady, worth twenty thousand pounds. Do you know any such person, madam?

Mel. Extravagant coxcomb! [*Aside.*] To be sure, a great many ladies of that fortune would be proud of the name of Mrs. Brazen.

Brazen. Nay, for that matter, madam, there are women of very good quality of the name of Brazen.

Enter WORTHY.

Mel. Oh, are you there, gentleman?—Come, captain, we'll walk this way. Give me your hand.

Brazen. My hand, heart's blood, and guts, are at your service. Mr. Worthy, your servant, my dear!

[Exit, leading MELINDA.

Wor. Death and fire! this is not to be borne!

Enter PLUME.

Plume. No more it is, 'faith.

Wor. What?

Plume. The March beer at the Raven. I have been doubly serving the king, raising men, and raising the excise. Recruiting and elections are rare friends to the excise.

Wor. You a'n't drunk?

Plume. No, no, whimsical only; I could be mighty foolish, and fancy myself mighty witty. Reason still keeps its throne, but it nods a little, that's all.

Wor. Then you're just fit for a frolic.

Plume. Just so.

Wor. Then recover me that vessel, from that Tangerine.

Plume. She's well rigged, but how is she manned?

Wor. By Captain Brazen, that I told you of to-day; she is called the Melinda, a first rate I can assure you; she sheered off with him just now, on purpose to affront me; but according to your advice I would take no notice, because I would seem to be above a concern for her behaviour; but have a care of a quarrel.

Plume. No, no; I never quarrel with any thing in my cups, but an oyster-wench, or a cookmaid, and if they ben't civil, I knock them down. But hearkye, my friend, I'll make love, and I must make love—I

39

tell you what, I'll make love like a platoon.

Wor. Platoon! how's that?

Plume. I'll kneel, stoop, and stand, 'faith: most ladies are gained by platooning.

Wor. Here they come; I must leave you.

[*Exit.*

Plume. So! now must I look as sober and demure as a whore at a christening.

Enter BRAZEN *and* MELINDA.

Brazen. Who's that, madam?

Mel. A brother officer of yours, I suppose, sir.

Brazen. Ay—my dear!

[*To* PLUME.

Plume. My dear!

[*Run and embrace.*

Brazen. My dear boy! how is't? Your name, my dear! If I be not mistaken, I have seen your face.

Plume. I never saw yours in my life, my dear——but there's a face well known as the sun's, that shines on all, and is by all adored.

Brazen. Have you any pretensions, sir?

Plume. Pretensions!

Brazen. That is, sir, have you ever served abroad?

Plume. I have served at home, sir, for ages served this cruel fair, and that will serve the turn, sir.

Mel. So, between the fool and the rake, I shall bring a fine spot of work upon my hands!

Brazen. Will you fight for the lady, sir?

Plume. No, sir, but I'll have her notwithstanding.

40

> *Thou peerless princess of Salopian plains,*
> *Envy'd by nymphs, and worshipp'd by the swains—*

Brazen. Oons, sir! not fight for her?

Plume. Pr'ythee be quiet—I shall be out—

> *Behold, how humbly does the Severn glide,*
> *To greet thee, princess of the Severn side.*

Brazen. Don't mind him, madam—if he were not so well dressed, I should take him for a poet; but I'll show you the difference presently. Come, madam, we'll place you between us, and now the longest sword carries her.

[*Draws.*

Mel. [*Shrieking.*]

Enter WORTHY.

Oh, Mr. Worthy! save me from these madmen!

[*Exit with* WORTHY.

Plume. Ha! ha! ha! why don't you follow, sir, and fight the bold ravisher?

Brazen. No, sir, you are my man.

Plume. I don't like the wages; I won't be your man.

Brazen. Then you're not worth my sword.

Plume. No; pray what did it cost?

Brazen. It cost me twenty pistoles in France, and my enemies thousands of lives in Flanders.

Plume. Then they had a dear bargain.

Enter SYLVIA, *in Man's Apparel.*

Syl. Save ye, save ye! gentlemen.

Brazen. My dear, I'm yours.

Plume. Do you know the gentleman?

41

Brazen. No, but I will presently—Your name, my dear?

Syl. Wilful, Jack Wilful, at your service.

Brazen. What, the Kentish Wilfuls, or those of Staffordshire?

Syl. Both, sir, both; I'm related to all the Wilfuls in Europe, and I'm head of the family at present.

Plume. Do you live in the country, sir?

Syl. Yes, sir, I live where I stand; I have neither home, house, or habitation, beyond this spot of ground.

Brazen. What are you, sir?

Syl. A rake.

Plume. In the army, I presume.

Syl. No, but I intend to list immediately. Lookye, gentlemen, he that bids the fairest, has me.

Brazen. Sir, I'll prefer you; I'll make you a corporal this minute.

Plume. Corporal! I'll make you my companion; you shall eat with me.

Brazen. You shall drink with me. Then you shall receive your pay, and do no duty.

Syl. Then you must make me a field-officer.

Plume. Pho, pho, pho! I'll do more than all this; I'll make you a corporal, and give you a brevet for serjeant.

Brazen. Can you read and write, sir?

Syl. Yes.

Brazen. Then your business is done—I'll make you chaplain to the regiment.

Syl. Your promises are so equal, that I'm at a loss to chuse. There is one Plume, that I hear much commended, in town; pray, which of you is Captain Plume?

Plume. I am Captain Plume.

Brazen. No, no, I am Captain Plume.

Syl. Heyday!

Plume. Captain Plume! I'm your servant, my dear!

Brazen. Captain Brazen! I'm yours—The fellow dares not fight. [*Aside.*

Enter KITE.

Kite. Sir, if you please———

[Goes to whisper PLUME.

Plume. No, no, there's your captain. Captain Plume, your serjeant has got so drunk, he mistakes me for you.

Brazen. He's an incorrigible sot. Here, my Hector of Holborn, here's forty shillings for you.

Plume. I forbid the bans. Lookye, friend, you shall list with Captain Brazen.

Syl. I will see Captain Brazen hanged first; I will list will Captain Plume: I am a free-born Englishman, and will be a slave my own way. Lookye, sir, will you stand by me?

[To BRAZEN.

Brazen. I warrant you, my lad.

Syl. Then I will tell you, Captain Brazen, [*To Plume.*] that you are an ignorant, pretending, impudent coxcomb.

Brazen. Ay, ay, a sad dog.

Syl. A very sad dog. Give me the money, noble Captain Plume.

Plume. Then you won't list with Captain Brazen?

Syl. I won't.

Brazen. Never mind him, child; I'll end the dispute presently. Harkye, my dear!

[*Takes* PLUME *to one Side of the Stage, and entertains him in dumb Show.*

Kite. Sir, he in the plain coat is Captain Plume; I am his serjeant, and will take my oath on't.

Syl. What! you are serjeant Kite?

43

Kite. At your service.

Syl. Then I would not take your oath for a farthing.

Kite. A very understanding youth of his age: but I see a storm coming.

Syl. Now, serjeant, I shall see who is your captain, by your knocking down the other.

Kite. My captain scorns assistance, sir.

Brazen. How dare you contend for any thing, and not dare to draw your sword? But you are a young fellow, and have not been much abroad; I excuse that; but pr'ythee, resign the man, pr'ythee do: you are a very honest fellow.

Plume. You lie; and you are a son of a whore.

> [*Draws, and makes up to* BRAZEN.

Brazen. Hold, hold; did not you refuse to fight for the lady?

> [*Retiring.*

Plume. I always do, but for a man I'll fight knee-deep; so you lie again.

> [PLUME *and* BRAZEN *fight a traverse or two about the Stage,* SYLVIA *draws, and is held by* KITE, *who sounds to Arms with his Mouth, takes* SYLVIA *in his Arms, and carries her off the Stage.*

Brazen. Hold! where's the man?

Plume. Gone.

Brazen. Then what do we fight for? [*Puts up.*] Now let's embrace, my dear!

Plume. With all my heart, my dear! [*Putting up.*] I suppose Kite has listed him by this time.

> [*Embraces.*

Brazen. You are a brave fellow: I always fight with a man before I make him my friend; and if once I find he will fight, I never quarrel with him afterwards. And now I'll tell you a secret, my dear friend! that lady we frightened out of the walk just now, I found in bed this morning, so beautiful, so inviting; I presently locked the door—but I'm a man of honour—but I believe I shall marry her nevertheless—her twenty

44

thousand pounds, you know, will be a pretty conveniency. I had an assignation with her here, but your coming spoiled my sport. Curse you, my dear, but don't do so again——

Plume. No, no, my dear! men are my business at present.

[*Exeunt.*

ACT IV.

SCENE I.

The Walk.

Enter ROSE *and* BULLOCK, *meeting.*

Rose. Where have you been, you great booby? you are always out of the way in the time of preferment.

Bul. Preferment! who should prefer me?

Rose. I would prefer you! who should prefer a man, but a woman? Come, throw away that great club, hold up your head, cock your hat, and look big.

Bul. Ah, Rouse, Rouse! I fear somebody will look big sooner than folk think of. Here has been Cartwheel, your sweetheart; what will become of him?

Rose. Lookye, I'm a great woman, and will provide for my relations: I told the captain how finely he played upon the tabor and pipe, so he sat him down for drum-major.

Bul. Nay, sister, why did not you keep that place for me? you know I have always loved to be a drumming, if it were but on a table, or on a quart pot.

Enter SYLVIA.

Syl. Had I but a commission in my pocket, I fancy my breeches would become me as well as any ranting fellow of them all; for I take a bold step, a rakish toss, and an impudent air, to be the principal ingredients in the composition of a captain. What's here? Rose, my nurse's daughter! I'll go and practise. Come, child, kiss me at once. [*Kisses her.*] And her brother too! Well, honest Dungfork, do you know the difference between a horse and a cart, and a cart-horse, eh?

Bul. I presume that your worship is a captain, by your clothes and your courage.

Syl. Suppose I were, would you be contented to list, friend?

Rose. No, no; though your worship be a handsome man, there be others as fine as you. My brother is engaged to Captain Plume.

47

Syl. Plume! do you know Captain Plume?

Rose. Yes, I do, and he knows me. He took the ribbands out of his shirt sleeves, and put them into my shoes: see there—I can assure you that I can do any thing with the captain.

Bul. That is, in a modest way, sir. Have a care what you say, Rouse; don't shame your parentage.

Rose. Nay, for that matter, I am not so simple as to say that I can do any thing with the captain but what I may do with any body else.

Syl. So!——And pray what do you expect from this captain, child?

Rose. I expect sir!—I expect—but he ordered me to tell nobody—but suppose he should propose to marry me?

Syl. You should have a care, my dear! men will promise any thing beforehand.

Rose. I know that; but he promised to marry me afterwards.

Bul. Wauns! Rouse, what have you said?

Syl. Afterwards! After what?

Rose. After I had sold my chickens—I hope there's no harm in that.

Enter PLUME.

Plume. What, Mr. Wilful so close with my market woman!

Syl. I'll try if he loves her. [*Aside.*] Close, sir, ay, and closer yet, sir. Come, my pretty maid, you and I will withdraw a little.

Plume. No, no, friend, I han't done with her yet.

Syl. Nor have I begun with her; so I have as good a right as you have.

Plume. Thou'rt a bloody impudent fellow!

Syl. Sir, I would qualify myself for the service.

Plume. Hast thou really a mind to the service?

Syl. Yes, sir, so let her go.

Rose. Pray, gentlemen, don't be so violent.

48

Plume. Come, leave it to the girl's own choice. Will you belong to me or to that gentleman?

Rose. Let me consider; you're both very handsome.

Plume. Now the natural inconstancy of her sex begins to work.

Rose. Pray, sir, what will you give me?

Bul. Dunna be angry, sir, that my sister should be mercenary, for she's but young.

Syl. Give thee, child! I'll set thee above scandal; you shall have a coach with six before and six behind; an equipage to make vice fashionable, and put virtue out of countenance.

Plume. Pho! that's easily done: I'll do more for thee, child, I'll buy you a furbelow-scarf, and give you a ticket to see a play.

Bul. A play! wauns! Rouse, take the ticket, and let's see the show.

Syl. Lookye, captain, if you won't resign, I'll go list with Captain Brazen this minute.

Plume. Will you list with me if I give up my title?

Syl. I will.

Plume. Take her; I'll change a woman for a man at any time.

Rose. I have heard before, indeed, that you captains used to sell your men.

Bul. Pray, captain, do not send Rouse to the Western Indies.

Plume. Ha! ha! ha! West Indies! No, no, my honest lad, give me thy hand; nor you nor she shall move a step farther than I do. This gentleman is one of us, and will be kind to you, Mrs. Rose.

Rose. But will you be so kind to me, sir, as the captain would?

Syl. I can't be altogether so kind to you; my circumstances are not so good as the captain's; but I'll take care of you, upon my word.

Plume. Ay, ay, we'll all take care of her; she shall live like a princess, and her brother here shall be—What would you be?

Bul. Oh, sir, if you had not promised the place of drum-major!

Plume. Ay, that is promised; but what think you of barrack-master? you are a person of understanding, and barrack-master you shall be—But what's become of this same Cartwheel you told me of, my dear?

Rose. We'll go fetch him—Come, brother barrack-master—We shall find you at home, noble captain?

[*Exeunt* ROSE *and* BULLOCK.

Plume. Yes, yes; and now, sir, here are your forty shillings.

Syl. Captain Plume, I despise your listing money; if I do serve, 'tis purely for love—of that wench, I mean—now let me beg you to lay aside your recruiting airs, put on the man of honour, and tell me plainly what usage I must expect when I am under your command?

Plume. Your usage will chiefly depend upon your behaviour; only this you must expect, that if you commit a small fault I will excuse it; if a great one I'll discharge you; for something tells me I shall not be able to punish you.

Syl. And something tells me that if you do discharge me 'twill be the greatest punishment you can inflict; for were we this moment to go upon the greatest dangers in your profession, they would be less terrible to me than to stay behind you—And now, your hand, this lists me— and now you are my captain.

Plume. Your friend. 'Sdeath! there's something in this fellow that charms me.

Syl. One favour I must beg—this affair will make some noise, and I have some friends that would censure my conduct, if I threw myself into the circumstance of a private centinel of my own head—I must therefore take care to be impressed by the act of parliament; you shall leave that to me.

Plume. What you please as to that—Will you lodge at my quarters in the mean time?

Syl. No, no, captain; you forget Rose; she's to be my bedfellow, you know.

Plume. I had forgot: pray be kind to her.

[*Exeunt severally.*

Enter MELINDA *and* LUCY.

Lucy. You are thoughtful, madam, am not I worthy to know the cause?

Mel. Oh, Lucy! I can hold my secret no longer. You must know, that hearing of a famous fortune-teller in town, I went disguised to satisfy a curiosity which has cost me dear. The fellow is certainly the devil, or one of his bosom-favourites: he has told me the most surprising things of my past life.

Lucy. Things past, madam, can hardly be reckoned surprising, because we know them already. Did he tell you any thing surprising that was to come?

Mel. One thing very surprising; he said, I should die a maid!

Lucy. Die a maid! come into the world for nothing!—Dear madam! if you should believe him, it might come to pass; for the bare thought on't might kill one in four and twenty hours—And did you ask him any questions about me?

Mel. You! why I passed for you.

Lucy. So 'tis I that am to die a maid—But the devil was a liar from the beginning; he can't make me die a maid—I've put it out of his power already. [*Aside.*

Mel. I do but jest. I would have passed for you, and called myself Lucy; but he presently told me my name, my quality, my fortune, and gave me the whole history of my life. He told me of a lover I had in this country, and described Worthy exactly, but in nothing so well as in his present indifference—I fled to him for refuge here to-day; he never so much as encouraged me in my fright, but coldly told me that he was sorry for the accident, because it might give the town cause to censure my conduct; excused his not waiting on me home, made me a careless bow, and walked off—'Sdeath! I could have stabbed him or myself, 'twas the same thing—Yonder he comes—I will so use him!

Lucy. Don't exasperate him; consider what the fortune-teller told you. Men are scarce, and as times go it is not impossible for a woman to die a maid.

Enter WORTHY.

Mel. No matter.

Wor. I find she's warned; I must strike while the iron is hot—You've a great deal of courage, madam, to venture into the walks where you were so lately frightened.

Mel. And you have a quantity of impudence, to appear before me, that you so lately have affronted.

Wor. I had no design to affront you, nor appear before you either, madam; I left you here because I had business in another place, and came hither thinking to meet another person.

Mel. Since you find yourself disappointed, I hope you'll withdraw to another part of the walk.

Wor. The walk is broad enough for us both.

[*They walk by one another, he with his Hat cocked, she fretting, and tearing her Fan; he offers her his Box, she strikes it out of his Hand; while he is gathering it up,* BRAZEN *enters, and takes her round the Waist; she cuffs him.*]

Brazen. What, here before me, my dear!

Mel. What means this insolence?

Lucy. Are you mad? don't you see Mr. Worthy?

[*To* BRAZEN.

Brazen. No, no; I'm struck blind—Worthy! odso! well turned—My mistress has wit at her fingers' ends—Madam, I ask your pardon; 'tis our way abroad—Mr. Worthy, you're the happy man.

Wor. I don't envy your happiness very much, if the lady can afford no other sort of favours but what she has bestowed upon you.

Mel. I'm sorry the favour miscarried, for it was designed for you, Mr. Worthy; and be assured 'tis the last and only favour you must expect at my hands——captain, I ask your pardon.

[*Exit with* LUCY.

Brazen. I grant it——You see, Mr. Worthy, 'twas only a random-shot; it might have taken off your head as well as mine. Courage, my dear! 'tis the fortune of war; but the enemy has thought fit to withdraw, I think.

Wor. Withdraw! Oons! sir, what d'ye mean by withdraw?

Brazen. I'll show you.

[*Exit.*

Wor. She's lost, irrecoverably lost, and Plume's advice has ruined me. 'Sdeath! why should I, that knew her haughty spirit, be ruled by a man that's a stranger to her pride?

Enter PLUME.

Plume. Ha! ha! ha! a battle royal! Don't frown so, man; she's your own, I'll tell you: I saw the fury of her love in the extremity of her passion. The wildness of her anger is a certain sign that she loves you to madness. That rogue, Kite, began the battle with abundance of conduct, and will bring you off victorious, my life on't: he plays his part admirably.

Wor. But what could be the meaning of Brazen's familiarity with her?

Plume. You are no logician, if you pretend to draw consequences from the actions of fools—Whim, unaccountable whim, hurries them on, like a man drunk with brandy before ten o'clock in the morning—— But we lose our sport; Kite has opened above an hour ago: let's away.

[*Exeunt.*

SCENE II.

A Chamber, a Table with Books and Globes.

KITE *disguised in a strange Habit, sitting at a Table.*

Kite. [*Rising.*] By the position of the heavens, gained from my observation upon these celestial globes, I find that Luna was a tide-waiter, Sol a surveyor, Mercury a thief, Venus a whore, Saturn an alderman, Jupiter a rake, and Mars a serjeant of grenadiers—and this is the system of Kite the conjurer.

Enter PLUME *and* WORTHY.

Plume. Well, what success?

Kite. I have sent away a shoemaker and a tailor already; one's to be a captain of marines, and the other a major of dragoons—I am to manage them at night——Have you seen the lady, Mr. Worthy?

53

Wor. Ay, but it won't do—Have you showed her her name, that I tore off from the bottom of the letter?

Kite. No, sir, I reserve that for the last stroke.

Plume. What letter?

Wor. One that I would not let you see, for fear that you should break windows in good earnest. Here captain, put it into your pocket-book, and have it ready upon occasion.

[*Knocking at the Door.*

Kite. Officers, to your posts. Tycho, mind the door.

[*Exeunt* PLUME *and* WORTHY.—SERVANT *opens the Door.*

Enter MELINDA *and* LUCY.

Kite. Tycho, chairs for the ladies.

Mel. Don't trouble yourself; we shan't stay, doctor.

Kite. Your ladyship is to stay much longer than you imagine.

Mel. For what?

Kite. For a husband—For your part, madam, you won't stay for a husband. [*To* LUCY

Lucy. Pray, doctor, do you converse with the stars, or the devil?

Kite. With both; when I have the destinies of men in search, I consult the stars; when the affairs of women come under my hands, I advise with my t'other friend.

Mel. And have you raised the devil upon my account?

Kite. Yes, madam, and he's now under the table.

Lucy. Oh, Heavens protect us! Dear madam, let's be gone.

Kite. If you be afraid of him, why do ye come to consult him!

Mel. Don't fear, fool: do you think, sir, that because I'm a woman I'm to be fooled out of my reason, or frighted out of my senses? Come, show me this devil.

Kite. He's a little busy at present, but when he has done he shall wait on

54

you.

Mel. What is he doing?

Kite. Writing your name in his pocket-book.

Mel. Ha! ha! my name! pray what have you or he to do with my name?

Kite. Lookye, fair lady! the devil is a very modest person, he seeks nobody unless they seek him first; he's chained up, like a mastiff, and can't stir unless he be let loose—You come to me to have your fortune told—do you think, madam, that I can answer you of my own head? No, madam; the affairs of women are so irregular, that nothing less than the devil can give any account of them. Now to convince you of your incredulity, I'll show you a trial of my skill. Here, you Cacodemo del Plumo, exert your power, draw me this lady's name, the word Melinda, in proper letters and characters of her own hand-writing—do it at three motions—one—two—three—'tis done—Now, madam, will you please to send your maid to fetch it?

Lucy. I fetch it! the devil fetch me if I do.

Mel. My name, in my own hand-writing! that would be convincing indeed!

Kite. Seeing is believing. [*Goes to the Table, and lifts up the Carpet.*] Here Tre, Tre, poor Tre, give me the bone, sirrah. There's your name upon that square piece of paper. Behold—

Mel. 'Tis wonderful! my very letters to a tittle!

Lucy. 'Tis like your hand, madam; but not so like your hand, neither; and now I look nearer 'tis not like your hand at all.

Kite. Here's a chambermaid now will outlie the devil!

Lucy. Lookye, madam, they shan't impose upon us; people can't remember their hands no more than they can their faces—Come, madam, let us be certain; write your name upon this paper, then we'll compare the two hands.

[*Takes out a Paper, and folds it.*

Kite. Any thing for your satisfaction, madam—Here is pen and ink.

[Melinda *writes*, Lucy *holds the Paper.*

Lucy. Let me see it, madam; 'tis the same—the very same—But I'll secure one copy for my own affairs. [*Aside.*

Mel. This is demonstration.

Kite. 'Tis so, madam—the word demonstration comes from Dæmon, the father of lies.

Mel. Well, doctor, I'm convinced: and now, pray, what account can you give of my future fortune?

Kite. Before the sun has made one course round this earthly globe, your fortune will be fixed for happiness or misery.

Mel. What! so near the crisis of my fate?

Kite. Let me see—About the hour of ten to-morrow morning you will be saluted by a gentleman who will come to take his leave of you, being designed for travel; his intention of going abroad is sudden, and the occasion a woman. Your fortune and his are like the bullet and the barrel, one runs plump into the other—In short, if the gentleman travels, he will die abroad, and if he does you will die before he comes home.

Mel. What sort of a man is he?

Kite. Madam, he's a fine gentleman, and a lover; that is, a man of very good sense, and a very great fool.

Mel. How is that possible, doctor?

Kite. Because, madam—because it is so—A woman's reason is the best for a man's being a fool.

Mel. Ten o'clock, you say?

Kite. Ten—about the hour of tea-drinking throughout the kingdom.

Mel. Here, doctor. [*Gives Money.*] Lucy, have you any questions to ask?

Lucy. Oh, madam! a thousand.

Kite. I must beg your patience till another time, for I expect more company this minute; besides, I must discharge the gentleman under the table.

Lucy. O, pray, sir, discharge us first!

56

Kite. Tycho, wait on the ladies down stairs.

[*Exeunt* MELINDA *and* LUCY.

Enter WORTHY *and* PLUME.

Kite. Mr. Worthy, you were pleased to wish me joy to-day; I hope to be able to return the compliment to-morrow.

Wor. I'll make it the best compliment to you that ever I made in my life, if you do; but I must be a traveller, you say?

Kite. No farther than the chops of the channel, I presume, sir.

Plume. That we have concerted already. [*Knocking hard.*] Heyday! you don't profess midwifery, doctor?

Kite. Away to your ambuscade.

[*Exeunt* WORTHY *and* PLUME.

Enter BRAZEN.

Brazen. Your servant, my dear?

Kite. Stand off, I have my familiar already.

Brazen. Are you bewitched, my dear?

Kite. Yes, my dear! but mine is a peaceable spirit, and hates gunpowder. Thus I fortify myself: [*Draws a Circle round him.*] and now, captain, have a care how you force my lines.

Brazen. Lines! what dost talk of lines! you have something like a fishing-rod there, indeed; but I come to be acquainted with you, man—What's your name, my dear?

Kite. Conundrum.

Brazen. Conundrum? rat me! I knew a famous doctor in London of your name—Where were you born?

Kite. I was born in Algebra.

Brazen. Algebra! 'tis no country in Christendom, I'm sure, unless it be some place in the Highlands in Scotland.

Kite. Right—I told you I was bewitched.

Brazen. So am I, my dear! I am going to be married—I have had two letters from a lady of fortune, that loves me to madness, fits, cholic, spleen, and vapours——shall I marry her in four and twenty hours, ay or no?

Kite. Certainly.

Brazen. Gadso, ay——

Kite.—Or no—but I must have the year and the day of the month when these letters were dated.

Brazen. Why, you old bitch! did you ever hear of love letters dated with the year and day of the month? do you think billetdoux are like bank bills?

Kite. They are not so good, my dear—but if they bear no date, I must examine the contents.

Brazen. Contents! that you shall, old boy! here they be both.

Kite. Only the last you received, if you please. [*Takes the Letter.*] Now, sir, if you please to let me consult my books for a minute, I'll send this letter enclosed to you with the determination of the stars upon it to your lodgings.

Brazen. With all my heart—I must give him—[*Puts his Hands in his Pockets.*] Algebra! I fancy, doctor, 'tis hard to calculate the place of your nativity—Here—[*Gives him Money.*] And, if I succeed, I'll build a watch-tower on the top of the highest mountain in Wales, for the study of astrology, and the benefit of the Conundrums.

[*Exit.*

Enter PLUME *and* WORTHY.

Wor. O doctor! that letter's worth a million; let me see it: and now I have it, I'm afraid to open it.

Plume. Pho! let me see it. [*Opening the Letter.*] If she be a jilt—Damn her, she is one—there's her name at the bottom on't.

Wor. How! then I'll travel in good earnest—By all my hopes, 'tis Lucy's hand.

Plume. Lucy's!

Wor. Certainly—'tis no more like Melinda's character, than black is to white.

Plume. Then 'tis certainly Lucy's contrivance to draw in Brazen for a husband—But are you sure 'tis not Melinda's hand?

Wor. You shall see; where's the bit of paper I gave you just now that the devil wrote Melinda upon?

Kite. Here, sir.

Plume. 'Tis plain they are not the same; and is this the malicious name that was subscribed to the letter which made Mr. Balance send his daughter into the country?

Wor. The very same: the other fragments I showed you just now.

Plume. But 'twas barbarous to conceal this so long, and to continue me so many hours in the pernicious heresy of believing that angelic creature could change. Poor Sylvia!

Wor. Rich Sylvia, you mean, and poor captain; ha! ha! ha!—Come, come, friend, Melinda is true, and shall be mine; Sylvia is constant, and may be yours.

Plume. No, she's above my hopes——but for her sake, I'll recant my opinion of her sex.

> *By some the sex is blam'd without design,*
> *Light harmless censure, such as yours and mine,*
> *Sallies of wit, and vapours of our wine:*
> *Others the justice of the sex condemn,*
> *And, wanting merit to create esteem,*
> *Would hide their own defects by censuring them:*
> *But they, secure in their all-conq'ring charms,*
> *Laugh at our vain attempts, our false alarms.*
> *He magnifies their conquests who complains,*
> *For none would struggle, were they not in chains.*

[*Exeunt.*

59

ACT V.

SCENE I.

Justice Balance's *House.*

Enter Balance *and* Scale.

Scale. I say, 'tis not to be borne, Mr. Balance.

Bal. Lookye, Mr. Scale, for my own part I shall be very tender in what regards the officers of the army—I only speak in reference to Captain Plume—for the other spark I know nothing of.

Scale. Nor can I hear of any body that does—Oh! here they come.

Enter Sylvia, Bullock, Rose, Prisoners, *and* Constable.

Const. May it please your worships, we took them in the very act, *re infecta*, sir—The gentleman, indeed, behaved himself like a gentleman, for he drew his sword and swore, and afterwards laid it down and said nothing.

Bal. Give the gentleman his sword again—Wait you without. [*Exeunt* Constable *and* Watch.] I'm sorry, sir, [*To* Sylvia.] to know a gentleman upon such terms, that the occasion of our meeting should prevent the satisfaction of an acquaintance.

Syl. Sir, you need make no apology for your warrant, no more than I shall do for my behaviour—my innocence is upon an equal foot with your authority.

Scale. Innocence! have you not seduced that young maid?

Syl. No, Mr. Goosecap, she seduced me.

Bul. So she did, I'll swear—for she proposed marriage first.

Bal. What, then you are married, child? [*To* Rose.

Rose. Yes, sir, to my sorrow.

Bal. Who was witness?

Bul. That was I—I danc'd, threw the stocking, and spoke jokes by their bedside, I'm sure.

Bal. Who was the minister?

Bul. Minister! we are soldiers, and want no minister—they were married by the articles of war.

Bal. Hold thy prating, fool——Your appearance, sir, promises some understanding; pray, what does this fellow mean?

Syl. He means marriage, I think—but that, you know, is so odd a thing, that hardly any two people under the sun agree in the ceremony; but among soldiers 'tis most sacred—our sword, you know, is our honour, that we lay down—the Hero jumps over it first, and the Amazon after —Leap, rogue; follow, whore—the drum beats a ruff, and so to bed: that's all: the ceremony is concise.

Bul. And the prettiest ceremony, so full of pastime and prodigality——

Bal. What! are you a soldier?

Bul. Ay, that I am—Will your worship lend me your cane, and I'll show you how I can exercise?

Bal. Take it. [*Strikes him over the Head.*]—Your name, pray, sir? [*To* Sylvia.

Syl. Captain Pinch: I cock my hat with a pinch, I take snuff with a pinch, pay my whores with a pinch; in short, I can do any thing at a pinch but fight.

Bal. And pray, sir, what brought you into Shropshire?

Syl. A pinch, sir: I know you country gentlemen want wit, and you know that we town gentlemen want money, and so——

Bal. I understand you, sir—Here, constable——

Enter Constable.

Take this gentleman into custody, till further orders.

Rose. Pray, your worship, don't be uncivil to him, for he did me no hurt; he's the most harmless man in the world, for all he talks so.

Scale. Come, come, child, I'll take care of you.

Syl. What, gentlemen, rob me of my freedom and my wife at once! 'tis the first time they ever went together.

Bal. Harkye, constable. [*Whispers him.*

Const. It shall be done, sir—come along, sir.

[*Exeunt* CONSTABLE, BULLOCK, *and* SYLVIA.

Bal. Come, Mr. Scale, we'll manage the spark presently.

[*Exeunt.*

SCENE II.

The Market Place.

Enter PLUME *and* KITE.

Plume. A baker, a tailor, a smith, butchers, carpenters, and journeymen shoemakers, in all thirty-nine—I believe the first colony planted in Virginia had not more trades in their company than I have in mine.

Kite. The butcher, sir, will have his hands full, for we have two sheep-stealers among us—I hear of a fellow, too, committed just now for stealing of horses.

Plume. We'll dispose of him among the dragoons—Have we never a poulterer among us?

Kite. Yes, sir, the king of the gipsies is a very good one; he has an excellent hand at a goose or a turkey—Here's Captain Brazen, sir. I must go look after the men.

Enter BRAZEN, *reading a Letter.*

Brazen. Um, um, um, the canonical hour——Um, um, very well—My dear Plume! give me a buss.

Plume. Half a score, if you will, my dear! What hast got in thy hand, child?

Brazen. 'Tis a project for laying out a thousand pounds.

Plume. Were it not requisite to project first how to get it in?

Brazen. You can't imagine, my dear, that I want twenty thousand pounds! I have spent twenty times as much in the service—But if this twenty thousand pounds should not be in specie——

Plume. What twenty thousand?

63

Brazen. Harkye—— [*Whispers.*

Plume. Married!

Brazen. Presently; we're to meet about half a mile out of town, at the waterside—and so forth—[*Reads.*] *For fear I should be known by any of Worthy's friends, you must give me leave to wear my mask till after the ceremony which will make me for ever yours.*—Lookye there, my dear dog!

[*Shows the Bottom of the Letter to* PLUME.

Plume. Melinda! and by this light her own hand! Once more, if you please, my dear—Her hand exactly—Just now, you say?

Brazen. This minute; I must be gone.

Plume. Have a little patience, and I'll go with you.

Brazen. No, no, I see a gentleman coming this way that may be inquisitive; 'tis Worthy, do you know him?

Plume. By sight only.

Brazen. Have a care, the very eyes discover secrets.

[*Exit.*

Enter WORTHY.

Wor. To boot and saddle, captain, you must mount.

Plume. Whip and spur, Worthy, or you won't mount.

Wor. But I shall; Melinda and I are agreed; she's gone to visit Sylvia, we are to mount and follow; and could we carry a parson with us, who knows what might be done for us both?

Plume. Don't trouble your head; Melinda has secured a parson already.

Wor. Already! do you know more than I?

Plume. Yes, I saw it under her hand—Brazen and she are to meet half a mile hence, at the waterside, there to take boat, I suppose, to be ferried over to the Elysian Fields, if there be any such thing in matrimony.

Wor. I parted with Melinda just now; she assured me she hated Brazen, and that she resolved to discard Lucy for daring to write letters to him in her name.

Plume. Nay, nay, there's nothing of Lucy in this—I tell ye, I saw Melinda's hand as surely as this is mine.

Wor. But I tell you, she's gone this minute to Justice Balance's country-house.

Plume. But I tell you, she's gone this minute to the waterside.

Enter a SERVANT.

Serv. Madam Melinda has sent word that you need not trouble yourself to follow her, because her journey to Justice Balance's is put off, and she's gone to take the air another way.   [*To* WORTHY.

Wor. How! her journey put off?

Plume. That is, her journey was a put off to you.

Wor. 'Tis plain, plain—But how, where, when is she to meet Brazen?

Plume. Just now, I tell you, half a mile hence, at the waterside.

Wor. Up or down the water?

Plume. That I don't know.

Wor. I'm glad my horses are ready—I shall return presently.

[*Exit.*

Plume. You'll find me at the Hall: the justices are sitting by this time, and I must attend them.

[*Exit.*

SCENE III.

A Court of Justice.

BALANCE, SCALE, *and* SCRUPLE, *upon the Bench*; CONSTABLE, KITE, MOB.

KITE *and* CONSTABLE *advance.*

Kite. Pray, who are those honourable gentlemen upon the bench?

Const. He in the middle is Justice Balance, he on the right is Justice Scale, and he on the left is Justice Scruple, and I am Mr. Constable;

four very honest gentlemen.

Kite. O dear, sir! I am your most obedient servant. [*Saluting the* Constable.] I fancy, sir, that your employment and mine are much the same; for my business is to keep people in order, and, if they disobey, to knock them down; and then we are both staff officers.

Const. Nay, I'm a serjeant myself—of the militia—Come, brother, you shall see me exercise. Suppose this a musket; now I'm shouldered.

[*Puts his Staff on his right Shoulder.*

Kite. Ay, you are shouldered pretty well for a constable's staff, but for a musket you must put it on the other shoulder, my dear!

Const. Adso! that's true—Come, now give the word of command.

Kite. Silence.

Const. Ay, ay, so we will—we will be silent.

Kite. Silence, you dog, silence!

[*Strikes him over the Head with his Halbert.*

Const. That's the way to silence a man with a witness. What do you mean, friend?

Kite. Only to exercise you, sir.

Const. Your exercise differs so much from ours, that we shall ne'er agree about it; if my own captain had given me such a rap, I had taken the law of him.

Enter Plume.

Bal. Captain, you're welcome.

Plume. Gentlemen, I thank you.

Scrup. Come, honest captain, sit by me. [Plume *ascends, and sits upon the Bench.*]—Now, produce your prisoners——Here, that fellow there, set him up. Mr. Constable, what have you to say against this man?

Const. I have nothing to say against him, an' please you.

Bal. No; what made you bring him hither?

66

Const. I don't know, an' please your worship.

Scale. Did not the contents of your warrant direct you what sort of men to take up?

Const. I can't tell, an' please ye; I can't read.

Scrup. A very pretty constable, truly. I find we have no business here.

Kite. May it please the worshipful bench, I desire to be heard in this case, as being the counsel for the king.

Bal. Come, serjeant, you shall be heard, since nobody else will speak; we won't come here for nothing.

Kite. This man is but one man, the country may spare him, and the army wants him; besides, he's cut out by nature for a grenadier; he's five feet ten inches high; he shall box, wrestle, or dance the Cheshire round with any man in the country; he gets drunk every Sabbath-day, and he beats his wife.

Wife. You lie, sirrah, you lie; an please your worship, he's the best natured pains-taking'st man in the parish, witness my five poor children.

Scrup. A wife and five children? you constable, you rogue, how durst you impress a man that has a wife and five children?

Scale. Discharge him, discharge him.

Bal. Hold, gentlemen. Harkye, friend, how do you maintain your wife and five children?

Plume. They live upon wild-fowl and venison, sir; the husband keeps a gun, and kills all the hares and partridges within five miles round.

Bal. A gun! nay if he be so good at gunning, he shall have enough on't. He may be of use against the French, for he shoots flying to be sure.

Scrup. But his wife and children, Mr. Balance?

Wife. Ay, ay, that's the reason you would send him away; you know I have a child every year, and you are afraid that they should come upon the parish at last.

Plume. Lookye there, gentlemen; the honest woman has spoke it at once; the parish had better maintain five children this year, than six or seven the next. That fellow, upon this high feeding, may get you two or three beggars at a birth.

Wife. Lookye, Mr. Captain, the parish shall get nothing by sending him away, for I won't lose my teeming-time, if there be a man left in the parish.

Bal. Send that woman to the house of correction,——and the man

——

Kite. I'll take care of him, if you please.

[*Takes him down.*

Scale. Here, you constable, the next. Set up that black-faced fellow, he has a gunpowder look; what can you say against this man, constable?

Const. Nothing, but that he's a very honest man.

Plume. Pray, gentlemen, let me have one honest man in my company, for the novelty's sake.

Bal. What are you, friend?

Mob. A collier; I work in the coal-pits.

Scrup. Lookye, gentlemen, this fellow has a trade, and the act of parliament here expresses, that we are to impress no man that has any visible means of a livelihood.

Kite. May it please your worship, this man has no visible means of a livelihood, for he works underground.

Plume. Well said, Kite; besides, the army wants miners.

Bal. Right, and had we an order of government for't, we could raise you in this and the neighbouring county of Stafford, five hundred colliers, that would run you under ground like moles, and do more service in a siege, than all the miners in the army.

Scrup. Well, friend, what have you to say for yourself?

Mob. I'm married.

Kite. Lack-a-day! so am I.

Mob. Here's my wife, poor woman.

Bal. Are you married, good woman?

Woman. I'm married in conscience.

Kite. May it please your worship, she's with child in conscience.

Scale. Who married you, mistress?

Woman. My husband: we agreed that I should call him husband, to avoid passing for a whore, and that he should call me wife, to shun going for a soldier.

Plume. A very pretty couple! What say you, Mr. Kite? will you take care of the woman?

Kite. Yes, sir, she shall go with us to the sea-side, and there, if she has a mind to drown herself, we'll take care nobody shall hinder her.

Bal. Here, constable, bring in my man.[*Exit* CONSTABLE.] Now, captain, I'll fit you with a man such as you never listed in your life.

Enter CONSTABLE *and* SYLVIA.

Oh, my friend Pinch! I'm very glad to see you.

Syl. Well, sir, and what then?

Scale. What then! is that your respect to the bench?

Syl. Sir, I don't care a farthing for you, nor your bench neither.

Scrup. Lookye, gentlemen, that's enough; he's a very impudent fellow, and fit for a soldier.

Scale. A notorious rogue, I say, and very fit for a soldier.

Const. A whoremaster, I say, and therefore fit to go.

Bal. What think you, captain?

Plume. I think he's a very pretty fellow, and therefore fit to serve.

Syl. Me for a soldier! send your own lazy lubberly sons at home; fellows that hazard their necks every day, in the pursuit of a fox, yet dare not peep abroad to look an enemy in the face.

Const. May it please your worships, I have a woman at the door to swear a rape against this rogue.

Syl. Is it your wife, or daughter, booby?

Bal. Pray, captain, read the articles of war; we'll see him listed immediately.

Plume. [Reads. *Articles of war, against mutiny and desertion, &c.*

Syl. Hold, sir——Once more, gentlemen, have a care what you do; for you shall severely smart for any violence you offer to me; and you, Mr. Balance, I speak to you particularly, you shall heartily repent it.

Plume. Lookye, young spark, say but one word more, and I'll build a horse for you as high as the cieling, and make you ride the most tiresome journey that ever you made in your life.

Syl. You have made a fine speech, good Captain Huff-cap! but you had better be quiet; I shall find a way to cool your courage.

Plume. Pray, gentlemen, don't mind him, he's distracted.

Syl. 'Tis false! I am descended of as good a family as any in your county; my father is as good a man as any upon your bench, and I am heir to twelve hundred pounds a-year.

Bal. He's certainly mad. Pray, captain, read the articles of war.

Syl. Hold, once more. Pray, Mr. Balance, to you I speak; suppose I were your child, would you use me at this rate?

Bal. No, 'faith: were you mine, I would send you to Bedlam first, and into the army afterwards.

Syl. But consider my father, sir; he's as good, as generous, as brave, as just a man as ever served his country; I'm his only child; perhaps the loss of me may break his heart.

Bal. He's a very great fool if it does. Captain, if you don't list him this minute, I'll leave the court.

Plume. Kite, do you distribute the levy money to the men, while I read.

Kite. Ay, sir. Silence, gentlemen!

[PLUME *reads the Articles of War.*

Bal. Very well; now, captain, let me beg the favour of you not to discharge this fellow, upon any account whatsoever. Bring in the rest.

70

Const. There are no more, an't please your worship.

Bal. No more! There were five, two hours ago.

Syl. 'Tis true, sir; but this rogue of a constable let the rest escape, for a bribe of eleven shillings a man, because he said the act allowed him but ten, so the odd shilling was clear gains.

All Just. How!

Syl. Gentlemen, he offered to let me go away for two guineas, but I had not so much about me: this is truth, and I am ready to swear it.

Kite. And I'll swear it: give me the book—'tis for the good of the service.

Mob. May it please your worship, I gave him half a crown, to say that I was an honest man; but now, since that your worships have made me a rogue, I hope I shall have my money again.

Bal. 'Tis my opinion, that this constable be put into the captain's hands, and if his friends don't bring four good men for his ransom by to-morrow night, captain, you shall carry him to Flanders.

Scale. Scrup. Agreed, agreed.

Plume. Mr. Kite, take the constable into custody.

Kite. Ay, ay, sir. [*To the* Constable.] Will you please to have your office taken from you? or will you handsomely lay down your staff, as your betters have done before you?

[Constable *drops his Staff.*

Bal. Come, gentlemen, there needs no great ceremony in adjourning this court. Captain, you shall dine with me.

Kite. Come, Mr. Militia Serjeant, I shall silence you now, I believe, without your taking the law of me.

[*Exeunt.*

SCENE IV.

A Room in Balance's *House.*

Enter Balance *and* Steward.

71

Stew. We did not miss her till the evening, sir; and then, searching for her in the chamber that was my young master's, we found her clothes there; but the suit that your son left in the press, when he went to London, was gone.

Bal. The white, trimm'd with silver?

Stew. The same.

Bal. You ha'n't told that circumstance to any body?

Stew. To none but your worship.

Bal. And be sure you don't. Go into the dining-room, and tell Captain Plume that I beg to speak with him.

Stew. I shall.

[*Exit.*

Bal. Was ever man so imposed upon! I had her promise, indeed, that she would never dispose of herself without my consent—I have consented with a witness, given her away as my act and my deed—and this, I warrant, the captain thinks will pass. No, I shall never pardon him the villany, first, of robbing me of my daughter, and then the mean opinion he must have of me, to think that I could be so wretchedly imposed upon: her extravagant passion might encourage her in the attempt, but the contrivance must be his. I'll know the truth presently.

Enter PLUME.

Pray, captain, what have you done with our young gentleman soldier?

Plume. He's at my quarters, I suppose, with the rest of my men.

Bal. Does he keep company with the common soldiers?

Plume. No, he's generally with me.

Bal. He lies with you, I presume?

Plume. No, 'faith; the young rogue fell in love with Rose, and has lain with her, I think, since she came to town.

Bal. So that between you both, Rose has been finely managed.

Plume. Upon my honour, sir, she had no harm from me.

Bal. All's safe, I find—Now, captain, you must know, that the young fellow's impudence in court was well grounded; he said I should heartily repent his being listed, and so I do, from my soul.

Plume. Ay! for what reason?

Bal. Because he is no less than what he said he was—born of as good a family as any in this county, and he is heir to twelve hundred pounds a-year.

Plume. I'm very glad to hear it—for I wanted but a man of that quality to make my company a perfect representative of the whole commons of England.

Bal. Won't you discharge him?

Plume. Not under a hundred pounds sterling.

Bal. You shall have it, for his father is my intimate friend.

Plume. Then you shall have him for nothing.

Bal. Nay, sir, you shall have your price.

Plume. Not a penny, sir; I value an obligation to you much above an hundred pounds.

Bal. Perhaps, sir, you shan't repent your generosity——Will you please to write his discharge in my pocket-book? [*Gives his Book.*] In the mean time, we'll send for the gentleman. Who waits there?

Enter STEWARD.

Go to the captain's lodging, and inquire for Mr. Wilful; tell him his captain wants him here immediately.

Serv. Sir, the gentleman's below at the door, inquiring for the captain.

Plume. Bid him come up. Here's the discharge, sir.

Bal. Sir, I thank you—'Tis plain he had no hand in't. [*Aside.*

Enter SYLVIA.

Syl. I think, captain, you might have used me better, than to leave me yonder among your swearing drunken crew; and you, Mr. Justice, might have been so civil as to have invited me to dinner, for I have eaten with as good a man as your worship.

73

Plume. Sir, you must charge our want of respect upon our ignorance of your quality—but now you are at liberty, I have discharged you.

Syl. Discharged me!

Bal. Yes, sir, and you must once more go home to your father.

Syl. My father! then I am discovered——Oh, sir! [*Kneeling.*] I expect no pardon.

Bal. Pardon! no, no, child; your crime shall be your punishment: here, captain, I deliver her over to the conjugal power, for her chastisement. Since she will be a wife, be you a husband, a very husband—When she tells you of her love, upbraid her with her folly; be modishly ungrateful, because she has been unfashionably kind; and use her worse than you would any body else, because you can't use her so well as she deserves.

Plume. And are you, Sylvia, in good earnest?

Syl. Earnest! I have gone too far to make it jest, sir.

Plume. And do you give her to me in good earnest?

Bal. If you please to take her, sir.

Plume. Why then I have saved my legs and arms, and lost my liberty; secure from wounds, I am prepared for the gout; farewell subsistence, and welcome taxes—Sir, my liberty and the hope of being a general, are much dearer to me than your twelve hundred pounds a-year—but to your love, madam, I resign my freedom, and, to your beauty, my ambition—greater in obeying at your feet, than commanding at the head of an army.

Enter WORTHY.

Wor. I am sorry to hear, Mr. Balance, that your daughter is lost.

Bal. So am not I, sir, since an honest gentleman has found her.

Enter MELINDA.

Mel. Pray, Mr. Balance, what's become of my cousin Sylvia?

Bal. Your cousin Sylvia is talking yonder with your cousin Plume.

Mel. and Wor. How!

Syl. Do you think it strange, cousin, that a woman should change; but I hope you'll excuse a change that has proceeded from constancy: I altered my outside, because I was the same within, and only laid by the woman, to make sure of my man: that's my history.

Mel. Your history is a little romantic, cousin; but since success has crowned your adventures, you will have the world on your side, and I shall be willing to go with the tide, provided you'll pardon an injury I offered you in the letter to your father.

Plume. That injury, madam, was done to me, and the reparation I expect, shall be made to my friend: make Mr. Worthy happy, and I shall be satisfied.

Mel. A good example, sir, will go a great way—When my cousin is pleased to surrender, 'tis probable I shan't hold out much longer.

Enter BRAZEN.

Brazen. Gentlemen, I am yours—Madam, I am not yours.

Mel. I'm glad on't, sir.

Brazen. So am I—You have got a pretty house here, Mr. Laconic.

Bal. 'Tis time to right all mistakes—My name, sir, is Balance.

Brazen. Balance! Sir, I am your most obedient—I know your whole generation—had not you an uncle that was governor of the Leeward Islands, some years ago?

Bal. Did you know him?

Brazen. Intimately, sir, he played at billiards to a miracle—You had a brother too, that was a captain of a fire-ship—poor Dick—he had the most engaging way with him of making punch—and then his cabin was so neat—but his poor boy Jack was the most comical bastard—Ha! ha! ha! ha! ha! a pickled dog, I shall never forget him.

Plume. Have you got your recruits, my dear?

Brazen. Not a stick, my dear!

Plume. Probably I shall furnish you, my dear! instead of the twenty thousand pounds you talked of, you shall have the twenty brave recruits that I have raised, at the rate they cost me——My commission I lay down, to be taken up by some braver fellow, that has more merit, and less good fortune—whilst I endeavour, by the example of this worthy gentleman, to serve my king and country at home.

> *With some regret I quit the active field,*
> *Where glory full reward for life does yield;*
> *But the recruiting trade, with all its train*
> *Of endless plague, fatigue, and endless pain,*
> *I gladly quit, with my fair spouse to stay,*
> *And raise recruits the matrimonial way.*   [*Exeunt omnes.*

Made in the USA
Coppell, TX
27 December 2023

26906029R00046